The Bramah Tea & Coffee Walk around London

Acknowledgements

I gratefully acknowledge all the materials, information and donations that have helped to make this book possible.

Firstly, from the trade and related associations in particular, I wish to thank: M.J. Bunston and Manuja Peiris (The International Tea Committee); Jim Devlin and Naomi Arnold (The Beverage Services Association); Pablo Dubois (The International Coffee Organisation); Michael P. Flynn (The Coffee Trade Association); William I.S. Gorman (The Tea Council); Barry Jaynes (The Tea Trade Benevolent Society of London) and Arun Kumar Sahu (The Tea Board of India).

Secondly, from the companies, I wish to thank in particular: Buchanan Butlers; Camellia plc; D.J.Miles; Rapido Coffee Services; Tetley GB Ltd; Warren Ford; Ujinotsuyu Seicha Co., Ltd; Wallingford Tea & Coffee Co. Ltd; The Windmill Tea Company and A.N. Woodhams and Co. Ltd.

I also want to record my gratitude to numerous friends who not only gave donations but also gave generously of their own valuable time. In particular, I should mention Kent Bakke; Michael Griffith; Mike Hinton; Arlyn J. Imberman; Akemi Osada; Don Riley; Stephen Traube and Hilary Wines. It is also important to recognise and record my thanks to all those people who have worked in the background providing support, in particular, Alan MacDougall, Penny Parkin and Susan Dixon.

Last, but not least, I wish to acknowledge the encouragement and counsel of the Trustees of the Bramah Tea and Coffee Museum Charitable Trust: Gordon Taylor, Betty Drew and Michael Bramah.

All of the assistance has been truly invaluable but any errors are entirely my own responsibility.

Edward Bramah

The Bramah Museum of Tea and Coffee,
40 Southwark Street, London, SE1 1UN
United Kingdom
Telephone/Fax: ++44 (0)20 7403 5650
E-mail: bramah@btconnect.com
www.bramahmuseum.co.uk
Copyright © Edward Bramah, 2005
ISBN 0-9550285-2-3
Published by Christian le Comte
www.christianlecomte.com
Edited & designed by Christian le Comte
Maps drawn by Draughtsman Ltd © Edward Bramah
Printed in China in November 2005
This book was set in ITC New Baskerville, an original design of John Baskerville, who not only excelled in the art of typography, but also stood out developing an extraordinary technique japanning tea trays.

The Bramah Tea &
Coffee Walk around London

*A guided tour of 400 years of tea and
coffee history around the City and Southwark*

by Edward Bramah

Christian le Comte
PUBLISHING

Contents

Advertisement for
Lipton's, 1893

HIGHEST
LIPTON'S D
Have gained the HIGHEST and (
WORLD'S
FROM THE T

1/-
FINEST TEA
No higher Price.
SPECIAL NOTICE.—*Delivered*
on orders of 5 lb.
LIPTON,
THE LARGEST TEA, COF
Sole Proprietor of the followi
Laymastotte, Monerakande, Mahalu
which cover thousands of acres of th

ONOURS.
:IOUS TEAS
ARD in the British Section at the
CHICAGO.
ENS·TO·THE·TEA·POT·

PER LB.
D CAN PRODUCE.
LB.   No higher Price.
tra **1d.** per lb. to any address in Great Britain
es sent free on application.
offee Planter, CEYLON.
SION DEALER IN THE WORLD.
nd Coffee Estates in Ceylon—Damⁱ atenne,
lle, Poopassie, Hanagalla, and Gigianella,
land in Ceylon.
IENA MILLS, CINNAMON GARDENS, COLOMBO.
STREET COLOMBO

Bland & Co's

Tasting's
of
39,000 packages of Tea for Sale.

on Tuesday 1st March 1842

at the London Commercial Sale Rooms
Mincing Lane

1 Hulbert 2 Ewart 3 Watkins 4 Moul 5 Thompson
6 Gibbs 7 Lloyd 8 Moffatt 9 Franks 10 George

Mess. Hulbert Lawson & Co

Bk & Sort	gy	tare	leaf	Col	quality	R	Sell
			Clifford				k
Con 1	50	25	blk & red wiry	M.	Bul 1. bl & fai str full bt	3	1
2	50	24	blk & red wir b	M.	Bul 1. bl & fai str ra P off	"	2
			Malcolm				
Hy 1	22	19	cld lis on bri	M.	Bul 1. ca strg	4	3
					bt @ Dec 15. 1837		
Hy 3	94	20	ca mix cld	M.	Bul 1. ca str lis coa	4	4
4	95	20	pa mix	M.	Bul 1. ca coarse	5	5
					bt Sep 2. 39		
Hy 1	41	19	dk ca bri	M.	Bul 1. ca str	6	6
2	19	18	mix & unev on bri	M.	Bul 1. ca coa	7	7
3	60	19	ca mix cuild	M.	Bul 1. ca coa bt	"	8
6	64	19	ca dull unev	M.	Bul 1. ca coarse	8	9
The Souchongs will be found					on page 4 by themselves		
			Ivanhoe				
Imp 1	208	5	even pa cuild	M.	Bul 1. coa & str Tu f	34	10
Gun 1	45	15	sml col & bri	M.	Bul 1. str coa bt	35	11
			Devonshire				
Bo 1	100	48 / 47	dull mix	1.	+ 1. coa faintish	38	12

Foreword

Dear Tea & Coffee Lover,

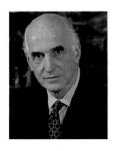

Edward Bramah,
founder and
director of the
Bramah Museum

Left: page of a
trader's notebook
of the London
Commercial Sale
Room auctions

It was in 1950 that I first visited a tea trading company at the corner of Eastcheap and Botolph Lane to arrange to work on a tea plantation in Central Africa. Subsequently I followed a double career in both tea and coffee and have visited many of the producing countries making friends all over the world.

My first love has always been that part of the City and Southwark where tea and coffee trading in Britain was established and carried on for over 350 years.

I have derived much personal pleasure researching and describing the history of tea and coffee in London as well as devising a walk that could be enjoyed either as a day out or, in parts, savoured within a brief hour.

It has been particularly pleasing both to witness and play a part in this history. From the austere post-war years to the present time we have seen a revolution in tea and coffee retailing and catering.

New shops and cafés abound across London to the vibrancy of the social and commercial life of the metropolis. It is thus my pleasure to share this book and its Walk around the City of London and Southwark, invite you to read it and enjoy the walking experience.

I look forward to welcoming you to the Bramah Museum and shop.

With all good wishes

Edward Bramah,
London 2005

E-mail: bramah@btconnect.com
www.bramahmuseum.co.uk

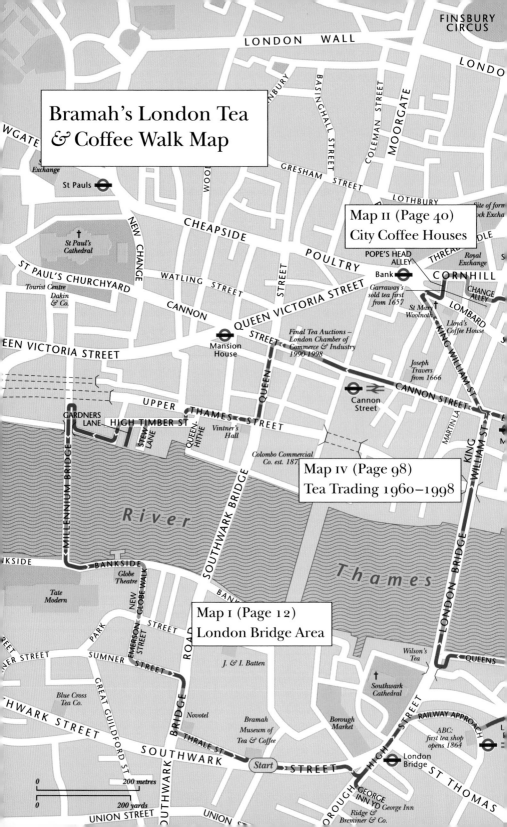

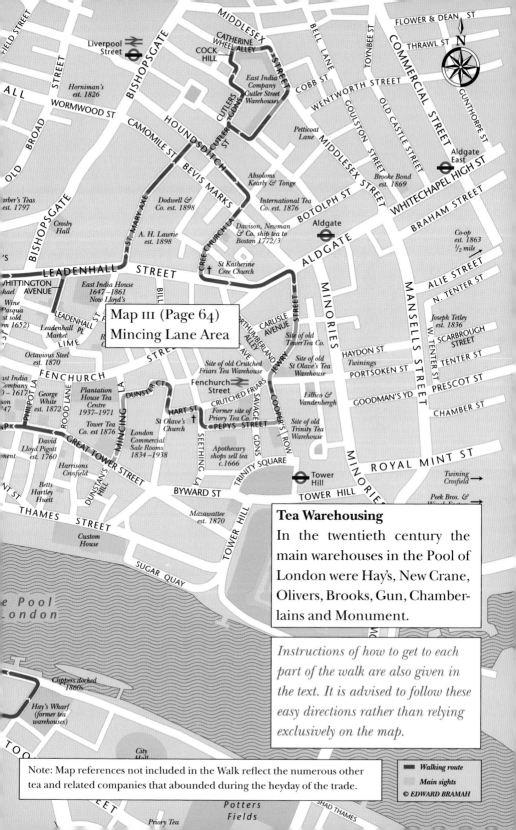

Liverpool Street

Map III (Page 64)
Mincing Lane Area

Tea Warehousing

In the twentieth century the main warehouses in the Pool of London were Hay's, New Crane, Olivers, Brooks, Gun, Chamberlains and Monument.

Instructions of how to get to each part of the walk are also given in the text. It is advised to follow these easy directions rather than relying exclusively on the map.

Note: Map references not included in the Walk reflect the numerous other tea and related companies that abounded during the heyday of the trade.

■■ *Walking route*
    Main sights
© *EDWARD BRAMAH*

Labels on map:

MIDDLESEX STREET
FLOWER & DEAN ST
CATHERINE WHEEL ALLEY
COCK HILL
BELL LANE
THRAWL ST
TOYNBEE ST
COMMERCIAL STREET
BISHOPSGATE
CUTLERS GDNS
CUTLER ST
East India Company Cutler Street Warehouses
COBB ST
WENTWORTH STREET
CUNTHORPE ST
Horniman's est. 1826
WORMWOOD ST
HOUNDSDITCH
CAMOMILE ST
Petticoat Lane
GOULSTON STREET
OLD CASTLE STREET
Brooke Bond est. 1869
Aldgate East
MIDDLESEX STREET
BOTOLPH ST
WHITECHAPEL HIGH ST
BRAHAM STREET
BEVIS MARKS
Absoloms Kearly & Tonge
ST MARY AXE
Dodwell & Co. est. 1898
International Tea Co. est. 1876
Davison, Newman & Co. ship tea to Boston 1772/3
Aldgate
Co-op est. 1863 ½ mile
ALIE STREET
N. TENTER ST
A. H. Lawrie est. 1898
CREE CHURCH LA
St Katherine Cree Church
Joseph Tetley est. 1836
W. TENTER ST
SCARBROUGH STREET
LEADENHALL STREET
BISHOPSGATE
Crosby Hall
arber's Teas est. 1797
WHITTINGTON AVENUE
hael
Wine Pasqua st sold m 1652)
East India House 1647–1861 Now Lloyd's
BILL
MINORIES
MANSELLS STREET
TENTER ST
LEADENHALL PL
Leadenhall Market
LIME STREET
CARLISLE AVENUE
Site of old Tower Tea Co.
HAYDON ST
PORTSOKEN ST
Twinings
PRESCOT ST
CHAMBER ST
Octavious Steel est. 1870
FENCHURCH
PORTNUMBERLAND ALLEY
HENRY STREET
Site of old St Olave's Tea Warehouse
GOODMAN'S YD
st India ompany 0–1617 son 47
PHILPOT LA
George White est. 1872
Plantation House Tea Centre 1937–1971
DUNSTER CT
Site of old Crutched Friars Tea Warehouse
Fenchurch Street
Lillico & Vandenbergh
COOPER'S LANE
SAVAGE GDNS
ROOD LANE
Tower Tea Co. est 1876
MINCING LA
HART ST
CRUTCHED FRIARS
SAVAGE GDNS
Site of old Trinity Tea Warehouse
David Lloyd Pigott est. 1760
GREAT TOWER STREET
St Olave's Church
London Commercial Sale Rooms 1834–1938
Former site of Priory Tea Co.
PEPYS STREET
Harrisons Crosfield
SEETHING LA
Apothecary shops sell tea c.1666
ROYAL MINT ST
Betts Hartley Huett
DUNSTAN'S HILL
BYWARD ST
TRINITY SQUARE
Tower Hill
Twining Crosfield
THAMES STREET
Mazawattee est. 1870
TOWER HILL
TOWER HILL
Peek Bros. & Winch Factory
Custom House
SUGAR QUAY
e Pool London
Clippers docked 1860s
Hay's Wharf (former tea warehouses)
City Hall
Potters Fields
Priory Tea
SHAD THAMES

1. The Bramah Museum

The walk begins and ends at the Bramah Museum of
Tea and Coffee, 40 Southwark Street, SE1 1UN, on the
southern side of the River Thames.

The Museum, which is only two minutes from London
Bridge Station, is the world's first museum devoted
entirely to the history of tea and coffee. It tells the
400 year commercial and social history of two of the
world's most important commodities.

*Tea caddy made by
Joseph Bramah,
c. 1760*

Since the British played a major role both in the
Chinese trade and in the development of production
in India, Ceylon and Africa, the Bramah Museum
naturally tells the story from a British perspective.
Through its ceramics, metalware, prints and displays,
the Museum also answers all those questions that
people from around the world ask about British tea
and coffee.

The creed of the Museum is that everything possible
should be done to maintain and improve the quality
of tea and coffee offered to the public. To this end,
tea seminars have been conducted here for more than
ten years.

*Bramah Museum
tea room*

The Bramah Museum of Tea and Coffee is a charitable foundation.

*Commemoration
800 cup teapot
made for the
Bramah Museum*

Edward Bramah examining a range of orthodox teas.

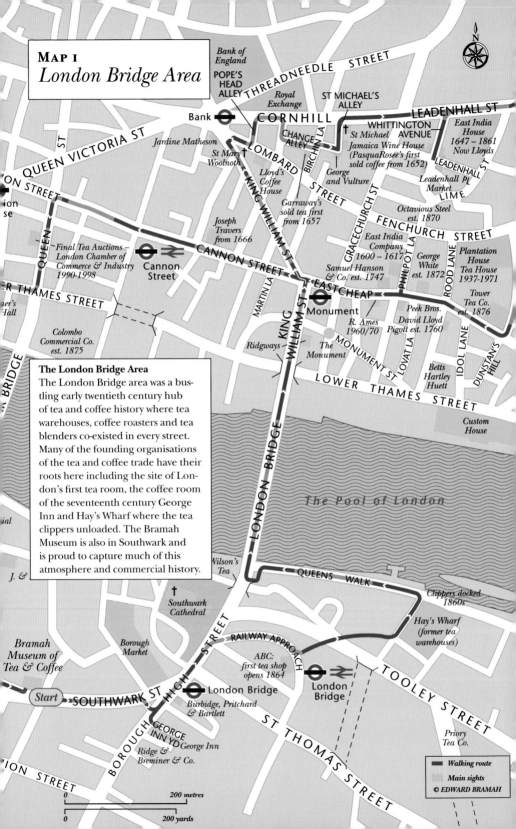

MAP I
London Bridge Area

THREADNEEDLE STREET

Bank of England

POPE'S HEAD ALLEY

ST MICHAEL'S ALLEY

Royal Exchange

Bank

CORNHILL

LEADENHALL ST

WHITTINGTON AVENUE

East India House 1647 – 1861 Now Lloyds

Jardine Matheson

CHANGE ALLEY

† St Michael

Jamaica Wine House (PasquaRosee's first sold coffee from 1652)

QUEEN VICTORIA ST

LOMBARD STREET

BIRCHIN LA

LEADENHALL ST

St Mary Woolnoth

George and Vulture

Leadenhall PL Market

ON STREET

Lloyd's Coffee House

KING WILLIAM ST

GRACECHURCH ST

Octavious Steel est. 1870

ion se

Garraway's sold tea first from 1657

FENCHURCH STREET

LIME

QUEEN

Joseph Travers from 1666

East India Company 1600 – 1617

George White est. 1872

Plantation House Tea House 1937-1971

Final Tea Auctions – London Chamber of Commerce & Industry 1990-1998

CANNON STREET

Samuel Hanson & Co. est. 1747

PHILPOT LA

ROOD LANE

Cannon Street

MARTIN LA

EASTCHEAP

Tower Tea Co. est. 1876

r THAMES STREET

KING WILLIAM ST

Monument

Peek Bros. David Lloyd Pigott est. 1760

R. Ames 1960/70

LOVAT LA

IDOL LANE

DUNSTAN'S HILL

er's Hall

Colombo Commercial Co. est. 1875

Ridgways

The Monument

MONUMENT ST

Betts Hartley Huett

The London Bridge Area

The London Bridge area was a bustling early twentieth century hub of tea and coffee history where tea warehouses, coffee roasters and tea blenders co-existed in every street. Many of the founding organisations of the tea and coffee trade have their roots here including the site of London's first tea room, the coffee room of the seventeenth century George Inn and Hay's Wharf where the tea clippers unloaded. The Bramah Museum is also in Southwark and is proud to capture much of this atmosphere and commercial history.

LOWER THAMES STREET

Custom House

The Pool of London

LONDON BRIDGE

Wilson's Tea

QUEENS WALK

Clippers docked 1860s

ial

Hay's Wharf (former tea warehouses)

J. &

† Southwark Cathedral

Bramah Museum of Tea & Coffee

Borough Market

HIGH STREET

RAILWAY APPROACH

TOOLEY STREET

ABC: first tea shop opens 1864

London Bridge

Start

SOUTHWARK ST

London Bridge

Priory Tea Co.

Burbidge, Pritchard & Bartlett

BOROUGH

GEORGE INN YD

George Inn

ST THOMAS STREET

Ridge & Breminer & Co.

ON STREET

0 — 200 metres

0 — 200 yards

■ Walking route

Main sights

© EDWARD BRAMAH

Tea and coffee arrive in England

We are often asked: 'Which came first to England, tea or coffee?'.
The answer is coffee, a claim substantiated by a reference in Evelyn's
diary of 1637, where we learn, that it was being taken by a member
of Balliol College, Oxford. This was followed by the opening of the
Oxford Coffee House called The Angel, in 1650.

London's first coffee house was opened in 1652. The African coffee,
brought up the Red Sea by dhow would have travelled overland via
Turkey to reach Britain across the English Channel. This was the
time when imagination was being fired by the discovery of new culi-
nary delights brought by ship from around the world.

The arrival of tea had a romance to it because it came from dis-
tant China, a mecca for explorers for centuries. The Portuguese,
who were the first to circumnavigate the Cape of Good Hope had
enjoyed in the 1500s a monopoly over the Far Eastern trade, but had
paid little attention to tea. It was subsequently introduced into Lis-
bon in 1600. The Dutch brought both Japanese and China tea back
from the Far East to Holland in 1610 and created a great elegance for
tea drinking. The London coffee house keepers would have heard
about the new drink in Holland and started to serve it in 1657. It is
most likely that their purchases came from ships' captains or from
the apothecary shops, where tea would have been sold as a tonic.
Any coffee house token, used to buy coffee of the period, would
confirm that the London coffee houses were in fact selling tea, coffee,
chocolate and sherbet, a popular syrup drink. However, with the
advent of the London Leisure Gardens, smuggling, the production of
ceramics, the Industrial Revolution, the tea auctions and the development of the Indian and Ceylon tea trades, Britain became the
greatest tea drinking nation of the world.

2. The George Inn

On leaving the Bramah Museum turn left into South-wark Street, passing the Hop Exchange at No 24 (the market for buying and selling hops which were used in making beer), built between 1863 and 1867. Have a look through the door at the imposing galleried trading area.

At the traffic lights, cross the road to the corner. Cross Borough High Street, turn right and turn into the George Inn Courtyard at No 77 Borough High Street.

Shield of The George Inn

It is most appropriate that your first call should be The George as it is the only example of a traditional galleried coaching inn remaining in London and has one of the last remaining old panelled coffee rooms.

The wooden high–back benches, tables and fire-place are typical of the period. The large wall clock would, no doubt, have reminded travellers of their coach departure times.

The inn is first recorded in 1542 but is almost cer-tainly older than that. The present inn was built in 1677. Charles Dickens enjoyed hospitality here. The atmosphere of the coffee rooms no doubt influ-enced Dickens's reference to tea making in *Oliver Twist*:

The George Inn courtyard

> …thrusting a silver spoon (private property) into the inmost recesses of a two–ounce tin tea–caddy, proceeded to make the tea […] The black teapot, being very small and easily filled, ran over while Mrs Corney was moralising; and the water slightly scalded Mrs Corney's hand.
>
> 'Drat the pot!' said the worthy matron, setting it down very hastily on the hob; 'a little stupid thing, that only holds a couple of cups! What use is it of, to anybody! Except,' said Mrs Corney, pausing, 'except to a poor desolate creature like me. Oh dear!'

The George Inn today.

Tea Shops and Tea Rooms

One would be very hard pressed to understand the difference between the tea shop and the tea room. Indeed many authors use the description when referring to the same kind of establishment simply to avoid repetition. In the early twentieth century, J. Lyons had the largest chain of tea establishments in the world and the English knew them as tea shops. Other companies such as Mecca, Kardomah, Express Dairy and many others also offered the same facilities, and called them either tea shops or tea rooms, frequently, the latter.

Ladies in the late eighteenth century would visit their favourite tea shops to examine teas and even enjoy sample tasting before making their purchase and the shops were clearly there in their day to sell retail. By the early 1900s, it was very much the thing for the upper classes to go to Gunter's or Rumplemeyer's for afternoon tea. These very exclusive tea shops were primarily confectioners. Gunter's for example, was famous for its ices, but the tea was served in the same way that Demels and Gerstner's in Vienna served coffee, as well as the most exquisite cakes in Europe.

Taking afternoon tea in Regent Street, London

In the period after World War II, because of the increased charges for rates and rent in London, it became very difficult to have specialist retail tea shops just serving and selling the teas. Such establishments therefore became a rarity. The author is of the opinion that, for people to learn how good the quality of both coffee and tea can be, it has to be demonstrated and what better way to do this than by serving enjoyable beverages in the tea and coffee room.

3. London's First Modern Tea Shop

Coming out of The George's courtyard, turn right and continue up Borough High Street past the Underground entrance and St Thomas Street which are both on your right until you reach Railway Approach. Opposite the London Bridge Station entrance is the site of what was the first modern tea shop opened by the Aerated Bread Company (ABC for short) in 1864.

'Nippy': the wait-resses for J Lyons nipped so quickly from table to table they were known as the 'nippies'.

Although baking bread was their main business initially, the manageress made a practice of sharing her pot of tea with customers. This proved so popular that she suggested that serving tea should become a regular part of their trade. The modern tea room was born, but alas, there is no plaque to mark the spot!

The London tea rooms, from the Victorian period onwards, were establishments where ladies coming to the West End to shop, could stop for afternoon tea and rest or talk with a friend. The Lyons' teashops, for instance, were renowned for their 'nippy' waitresses who were always smartly dressed in a starched collar, aprons and caps.

A typical ABC shop

Lyons' Company distribution cart

Interior view of the coffee room in the London Bridge Railway Terminus Hotel, c. 1860.

Tea Clippers

Down through the years, Londoners have shared with
New Yorkers the excitement of witnessing the arrival
of great and innovative sailing ships from around the
world. The UK and USA have produced between them
the finest sailing ships ever to grace the seas: the tea
clippers.

For nearly two hundred years, the ships of the East
India Company, known as tea wagons, were built for
both cargo and passengers. It used to take a year for
the ships to get to China and nearly a year to come
back again. The first suggestion of change in ship
design came from a ship's owner in America,
Edward Knight Collins, with ambition to make
ships that would sail faster and therefore be
more profitable.

In India, however, another trade
was calling for more speed. The
owners of ships carrying opium
from India to China saw
the chance to double or
triple their profits

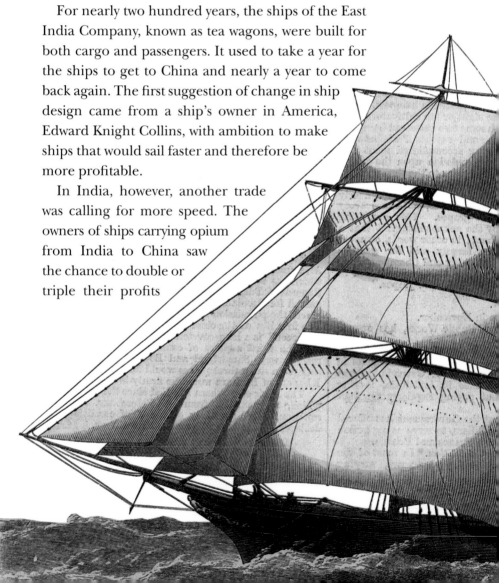

if they could sail against the monsoon two or three times a year, rather than once. To do this, ships were required which could cut through the water with a sharp bow, narrow hulls, tilted masts, and the most efficient rigs for beating to windward.

The Tea clipper Spindrift, winner of the tea race from China, 1868

The clippers were long and narrow ships built with u–shaped bottoms for speed and able to carry a large area of sail with three masts. They required strong-willed captains to drive them speedily, yet safely.

The first British tea clipper was the *Storno-way*, built in Aberdeen in 1850. Sixteen years later, many clippers took part in the greatest sailing race of all time, when 12 ships sailed from Foochow to London. The *Taeping, Ariel* and *Serica* all docked in London after 99 days sailing on the same tide. The *Taeping* berthed at the London docks, just below Tower Bridge, on the north side of the river.

4. Hay's Wharf

Continue by walking to the entrance of London Bridge station. By the left of the gateway for platforms 1 to 6 is a foot bridge, which takes you over Tooley Street, and down an escalator. Directly opposite the escalator is a passageway to Hay's Galleria. This transformation from a wharf into a shopping area, complete with glass vaulted roof, was finished in 1988.

Hay's Wharf with carts being loaded

Although Hay's Wharf accommodated the constant arrival of barges bringing teas off–loaded from ships lower down the river, it received fame in the 1860s by being able to berth some of the famous tea clippers which had raced from China with the new season's tea.

Tea clippers could unload as much as 14,000 chests of tea in a mere 30 hours. Thus, if they docked at 4 AM, for example, they could have discharged their cargo by 10 AM the next morning.

View of Hay's Wharf in 1857

At the River Thames end of Hay's Galleria turn left along Queens Walk which will lead you to the steps that will take you up onto London Bridge where you turn right to cross over the bridge.

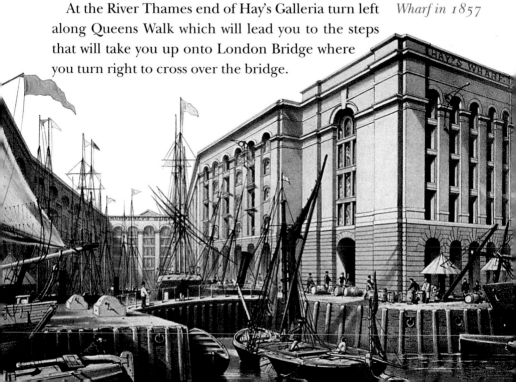

Hay's Wharf has been refurbished and converted into Hay's Galleria.

5. The Pool of London

As you cross London Bridge, on your right is the Pool of London, where ships in the seventeenth and eighteenth centuries unloaded their cargoes by the Custom

Above: the landing of passengers and cargo from France at Custom House, 1757

House. The present Custom House (see pages 32–33) is the nineteenth-century low grey building with trees in front of it on the north shore. This seemed to be conveniently situated next to the Tower of London to ensure the tax authorities received their money.

Above left: view of the Pool of London with Custom House and the Tower of London, 1840

Later, many of the East India ships, clippers (1850–90), and steam ships used to unload their cargoes down river, with the goods being brought to the warehouses by barges or by road. With so much food being warehoused in the area it became known as London's Larder.

Tea broker taking samples on board a tea ship in the London docks

View of the Pool of London today.

Tea and Health

While it is true that the wealthy took to the fashion
of drinking tea and led the trend, the initial impetus
for tea drinking came about through a major disaster.
One thing led to another. In 1665, the concentration
of coffee houses, where tea had been introduced,
was in the City. It was here that the Great Plague, in
which 70,000 to 100,000 Londoners died in a year,
broke out. The death toll of one in five, as Samuel
Pepys records in his diary 'was a terribly frightening
experience',but equally so must have been the catas-
trophe of the Great Fire of London the following year,
as it swept away all property from London Bridge to
Fleet Street. Coming immediately after the plague,
you can surely imagine people wondering, for health

reasons alone, why they should not let the whole City burn, so that the City could be built again.

The next year, women found there was nowhere for their children to play because the City was being rebuilt in brick and stone. One can imagine the women pleading with their husbands to take their children to the leisure gardens recently opened by entrepreneurs. Here families could spend more time in the open far away from the fetid air of the City.

The Great Fire of London, 1666

Once people arrived at the leisure gardens they were undoubtedly tired, and it became fashionable to ask to be served with the new tea drink from China. People knew that to make tea, the water had to be freshly boiled, and that made it a safe drink. In fact, over 700 years before, tea was considered to be so health-giving that it was used to combat the plague in Japan.

6. The Monument

London Bridge leads into the first part of King William Street, named after William IV, which was cut through from the Royal Exchange to London Bridge between 1829 and 1835. On the right, before reaching The Monument (close to the present Adelaide House), Thomas Ridgway opened a shop retailing tea in 1836.

View of The Monument showing the busy streets in the City, c. 1752

The grandeur of the tea merchants' buildings indicates what a prosperous trade it was.

The Monument was built to commemorate the Great Fire of London in 1666 according to the designs of Sir Christopher Wren. Adjacent to The Monument is Eastcheap (see also page 94). In 1836 there were five retail tea merchants and coffee dealers and sixty–four tea and coffee merchants.

Ridgway, 4 & 5 King William Street

View of The Monument today.

Smuggling

The first China teas, brought into this country by the East India Company, were mostly high quality green teas, although black China teas from the Bohea Hills gained rapid popularity and both fetched up to 30 shillings (£1.50) per pound.

Between 1660 and 1760, £1 was worth approximately £70 to £80 at current values

The Government saw in tea a marvellous source of revenue. In the hundred years between 1711 and 1810, £77 million duty was collected on tea, and duties ranged from 12.5% to 200%. As a result, trading in smuggled tea flourished in the eighteenth century. The challenge of bringing tea into England without paying import duty was an activity that most people did not regard as criminal.

In 1720, the Ostend Company smuggled tea with ships owned by London merchants and commanded by British companies. The officers and men of the East India Company's ships were

bringing home privately bought tea from the East. The East India ships were watched closely by the revenue service as they anchored.

Despite the passing of laws to prohibit tea from being imported into England from other parts of Europe, by the 1760s smuggling had grown into a highly organised commercial enterprise, centred around the isolated coastline of Southern England. Smuggled tea accounted for over half of the trade and was threatening the legitimate business.

In 1784, the Commutation Act was brought in under William Pitt. It cut taxation from 119% to 12.5% and put the smugglers out of business, but not before they had helped popularise the tea habit in all social classes.

Even the smugglers stopped for tea

7. Custom House

On the river, beyond the bottom of Monument Street, is the Custom House. You have already seen the Custom House from the Thames (see page 24), so there is no need to visit it on this walk, but it is worth providing some facts. It has occupied the site since Anglo–Saxon times with new buildings in 1272, 1668 and 1825.

Interior view of the Long Room in the Custom House, 1808

At the Custom House, in the busy Long Room, merchants had to process the clearing of their goods. Captains from all over the world had to come here to get the release certificates to be able to sell their cargoes. Thus in effect, it became one of the first trading floors in London. Defoe described the famous room as the 'best meeting place in Europe'.

Custom House today with the Swiss Re Tower behind it.

8. St Mary Woolnoth Church

Resume your walk until you arrive at the end of King William Street; just before reaching Bank Station, to your right you will see St Mary Woolnoth Church. If the church is open, you will be able to see the plaque on the right hand wall to commemorate the life of Edward Lloyd whose coffee house was just around the corner in Lombard Street. This street was also the home of famous tea company Jardine Matheson whose ship, *Sarah*, carried the first cargo of 'free' tea from China to London following the end of the East India Company's monopoly.

Plaque indicating the site of Jonathan's Coffee House in Change Alley

Jonathan's Coffee House, 1763

In this immediate vicinity of Cornhill there were no fewer than fifteen coffee houses established before 1700. Although most were destroyed in the Great Fire of 1666 and by fire again in 1748, they were rebuilt. Eastern in origin, the coffee houses had a natural simplicity. Apart from providing a refuge from Britain's inclement weather, the companionship within, undoubtedly fed the mind as the coffee fed the body. There are entries in the register of St Mary Woolnoth of the servants of Jonathan Miles, a Coffeeman (possibly the owner of Jonathan's Coffee House), who were buried there.

Tablet erected in memory of Edward Lloyd

St Mary Woolnoth Church, 1832.

Business in the Coffee Houses

Pasqua Rosee's coffee house (see page 54) heralded a
fashion that percolated into every street and alleyway.
In so doing, it greatly influenced the lives and habits
of the city merchants, particularly those in the neigh-
bourhood of the Royal Exchange, which was the centre
of London commerce.

*Politicians in
a coffee house,
1762*

Into the coffee houses came men of many trades
and callings to discuss their deals and sales over a hot
drink, knowing that the men they wished to meet
would be there also. Some of our greatest modern commercial institutions started life inside coffee houses.

Towards the end of the seventeenth century the
stockbrokers deserted the Royal Exchange for the
coffee houses.

Coffee houses did not have everything their own
way however. Some city traders complained bitterly
about the new and (to them) obnoxious smell that
came from the roasting of beans by night and day.

Most alarmed, somewhat naturally because of the
fire risk, were the booksellers. Alehouse keepers were
also loud in their complaints, fearing that their trade

Coffee and tea grocers, 1805

would decline from the new competition. In fact they encouraged such detrimental descriptions of coffee as 'syrup and soot' and 'essence of old shoes'.

Even the tragedy of the Great Plague of 1665 could not dampen the popularity of the coffee houses, though in those dangerous times a customer on arrival would be closely questioned concerning the health of his family.

After the Great Fire of the following year, the coffee houses were among the first buildings to reappear in the City. Their rapid growth, over the next fifty years, from the vicinity of the Royal Exchange and Fleet Street to Bishopsgate, Charing Cross, the Strand, Southwark and the Barbican and from Westminster down to St James's, provided ample proof of their necessity to the business community. They were also the kingpins on which the social life of the City revolved.

The Coffee-house Politicians: an interior view of a London Coffee-house with clients absorbed in newspapers and in conversation, 1772

The Interior of a Coffee House

This picture shows an up–market coffee house on a slack day in about 1705. Patrons served at long tables are smoking, and generally enjoying their coffee served in cups without handles. The coffee would be made from water in the hanging kettle and kept hot by a blazing fire.

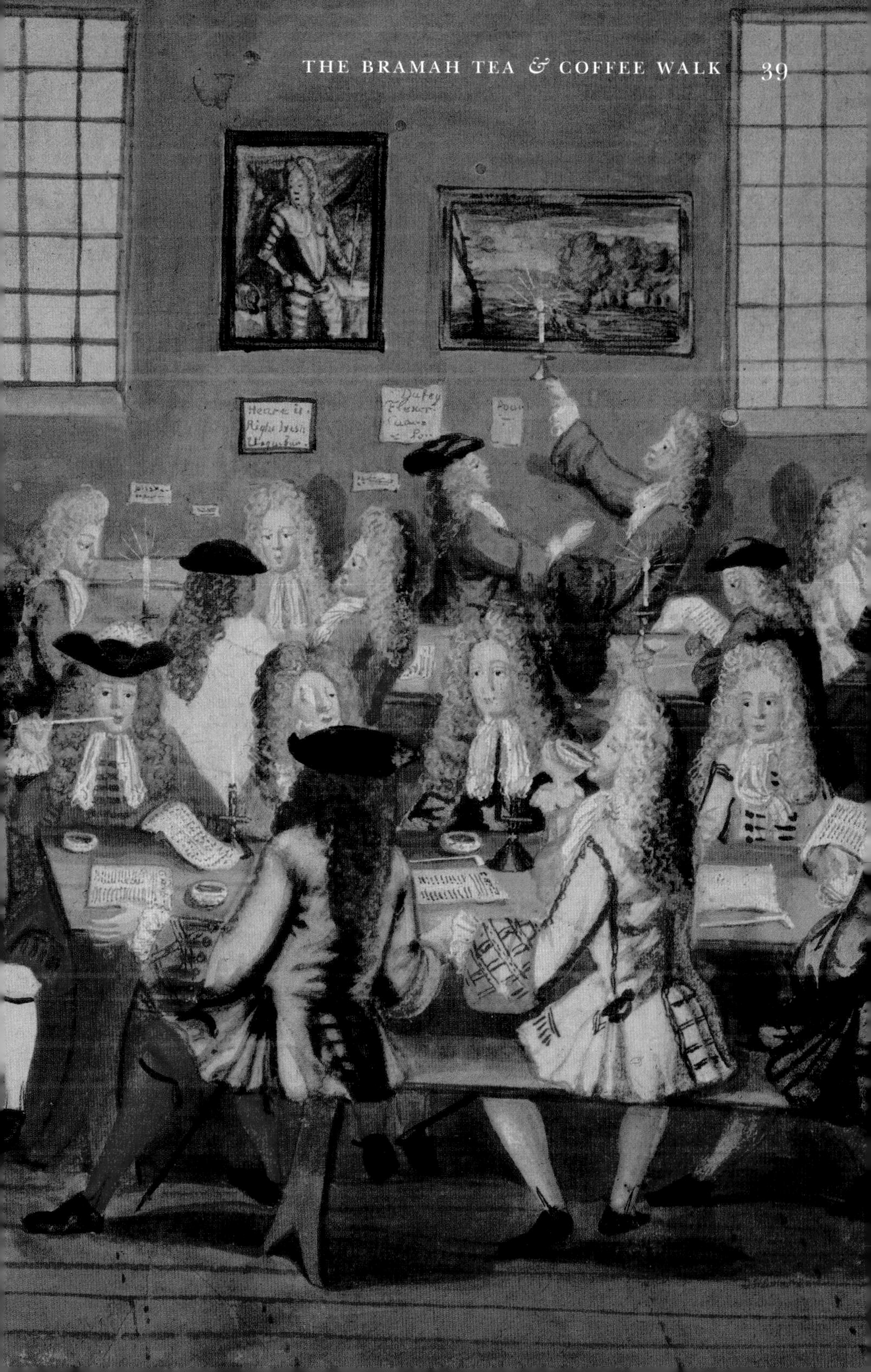

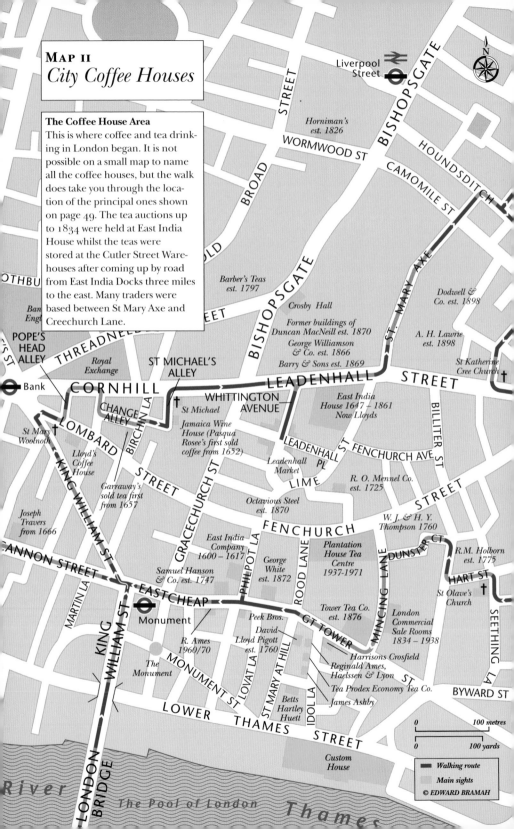

MAP II
City Coffee Houses

The Coffee House Area
This is where coffee and tea drinking in London began. It is not possible on a small map to name all the coffee houses, but the walk does take you through the location of the principal ones shown on page 49. The tea auctions up to 1834 were held at East India House whilst the teas were stored at the Cutler Street Warehouses after coming up by road from East India Docks three miles to the east. Many traders were based between St Mary Axe and Creechurch Lane.

Liverpool Street

BISHOPSGATE

Horniman's est. 1826

WORMWOOD ST

HOUNDSDITCH

CAMOMILE ST

BROAD

OLD

BISHOPSGATE

ST. MARY AXE

Dodwell & Co. est. 1898

OTHBU

Ban
Engl

Barber's Teas est. 1797

Crosby Hall

Former buildings of
Duncan MacNeill est. 1870
George Williamson & Co. est. 1866
Barry & Sons est. 1869

A. H. Lawrie est. 1898

POPE'S HEAD ALLEY

THREADNEEDLE

Royal Exchange

ST MICHAEL'S ALLEY

St Katherine Cree Church

Bank

CORNHILL

CHANGE ALLEY

BIRCHIN LA

† St Michael

WHITTINGTON AVENUE

LEADENHALL STREET

East India House 1647 – 1861 Now Lloyds

BILLITER ST

St Mary Woolnoth

LOMBARD

Jamaica Wine House (Pasqua Rosee's first sold coffee from 1652)

LEADENHALL PL

ST FENCHURCH AVE

Lloyd's Coffee House

Leadenhall Market

Garraway's sold tea first from 1657

STREET

GRACECHURCH ST

LIME

R. O. Mennel Co. est. 1725

STREET

Joseph Travers from 1666

KING WILLIAM ST

Octavious Steel est. 1870

FENCHURCH

W. J. & H. Y. Thompson 1760

East India Company 1600 – 1617

PHILPOT LA

George White est. 1872

Plantation House Tea Centre 1937-1971

DUNSTER CT

R.M. Holborn est. 1775

CANNON STREET

MARTIN LA

Samuel Hanson & Co. est. 1747

EASTCHEAP

ROOD LANE

Tower Tea Co. est. 1876

MINCING LANE

HART ST

St Olave's Church †

Monument

Peek Bros.

GT TOWER

London Commercial Sale Rooms 1834 – 1938

SEETHING LA

R. Ames 1960/70

KING WILLIAM ST

The Monument

MONUMENT ST

David Lloyd Pigott est. 1760

LOVAT LA

ST MARY AT HILL

Betts Hartley Huett

IDOL LA

Harrisons Crosfield
Reginald Ames,
Haelssen & Lyon
Tea Prodex Economy Tea Co.

James Ashby

BYWARD ST

LONDON BRIDGE

LOWER THAMES STREET

Custom House

0   100 metres
0   100 yards

━━ Walking route
     Main sights
© EDWARD BRAMAH

River   The Pool of London   Thames

The rules of a Coffee House

The Rules and Orders of the Coffee House around 1670 from Ukers's *All about Coffee*, published 1935.

Enter, Sirs, freely, but first, if you please,
Peruse our civil orders, which are these.
First, gentry, tradesmen, all are welcome hither,
And may without a front sit down together:
Pre–eminence of place none here should mind,
But take the next fit seat that he can find:
Nor need any, if finer persons come, rise up to assign to them his room;
To limit men's expense, we think not fair,
But let him forfeit twelve–pence that shall swear;
He that shall any call here begin,
Shall give each man a dish t'atone the sin;
And so shall he, whose compliments extend
So far to drink in coffee to his friend;
Let noise of loud disputes be quiet forborne,
No maudlin lovers here in corners mourn,
But all be brisk and talk, but not too much,
On sacred things, that none presume to touch.
Nor profane scriptures, nor saucily wrong affairs of state with an
irreverent tongue:
Let mirth be innocent, and each man see that all his jests without
reflection be;
To keep the house more quiet and from blame, we banish hence
cards, dice, and every game; nor can allow of wages that exceed
Five shillings, which oft times much trouble breed;
Let all that's lost or forfeited be spent
In such good liquor as the house doth vent.
And customer's endeavour, to their powers
For to observe still, seasonal hours.
Lastly, that each man what he calls for pay,
And so you are welcome to come every day.

9. Lloyd's Coffee House

On leaving St Mary Woolnoth, turn sharp right into Lombard Street, named after Italian bankers who settled here from Lombardy in the thirteenth century; you will see a plaque set into the wall on the right to mark the site of Lloyd's Coffee House from 1691 to 1785.

The development of the coffee houses did much to help the traders and Lloyd's especially assisted those in marine insurance, where men with a common trading interest could meet conveniently but briefly. Policy brokers of the seventeenth century, seeking subscribers, found the coffee houses invaluable.

Lloyd's was next to the General Post Office and had a successful private arrangement for obtaining the shipping lists (sailing schedules) from the Postmaster General. This coffee house is the origin of the modern Lloyd's insurance market.

The advertisement for Lloyd's Coffee House on the next page taken from the *Daily Gazetteer*, 27 August 1746, announces 'sales by the candle'. These were auctions during which bids were received only so long as a small piece of candle burned.

Entrance to Pope's Head Alley (see page 44)

Advertisements for inclusion in this newspaper were received at Sam's Coffee House, near Custom House (see bottom of page 49 for location of Sam's Coffee House).

Advertisements in the Daily Gazetteer

Now retrace your steps back down Lombard Street almost to the end.

For Sale by the CANDLE,

AT the MARINE Coffee-House in Birchin-Lane, Cornhill, some Time next Week;

Tea,
Martinico Coffee,
Mocha, ditto,
Cocoa Nutts, at constant Price,
Marriacabo, ditto,
Sago,
Sweet Almonds,
Fine Cinnamon Cassia,
Anniseeds,
Pistachia Nuts,
Salt Petre,
Soap,
Turmerick,
Gum Arabaek,
Verdigreece,
Aqua Fortis,
Argol,

Cream of Tartar,
Leghorn and Chip Hats,
Juniper Berries,
Manna,
Isonglass,
Opium,
Myrrh,
Bees Wax, in Time,
Assafætida,
China Mosch,
New England Castor,
Rhubarb,
Hungary Water,
Cubebs,
Gum Sandrack,
And sundry other Goods.

Catalogues will be timely dispersed by

WILLIAM HOMER, Broker.

For Sale by the CANDLE,

At LLOYD's Coffee-House, in Lombard-Street, on WEDNESDAY the TENTH of SEPTEMBER, 1746, at TWELVE o'Clock at Noon

THE SANDWICH Snow Privateer, with 14 Carriage Guns, Six and Four Pounders, an exceeding fine Sailer, Plantation built, about Two Years old, Burthen about 130 Ton, with a very good Inventory, and may be fitted to Sea at a small Expence, now lying on the Mud near Gun Dock, Wapping, Capt. THOMAS PALGRAVE, Commander.

Inventories of the said Snow will be timely delivered by

CHARLES ROGERS, Broker, over-against Lloyd's Coffee-House.

10. Change Alley

Crossing Lombard Street you will come to Pope's Head Alley where, from 1771 to 1774, Lloyd's provided room for its members. The alley is at present closed for building work, but is due to reopen in 2006. During the building work just walk to the end of Lombard Street and turn right into Cornhill where you see the

Street scene in Change Alley depicting events surrounding the South Sea Bubble of 1720. The scene is taking place in front of Garraway's Coffee House and a pawn shop.

Royal Exchange. The alley, a short cut to Cornhill, leads to the Royal Exchange, which was built in 1844. Although the original Exchange was founded in 1566 as a centre for every kind of commerce, specialist traders started to go to the nearby coffee houses to enjoy more privacy for their dealings.

With the Royal Exchange on your left, walk up Cornhill; on your right is Change Alley (formerly Exchange Alley). As you go in, immediately on either side of the alley is the site where the New Union and Union coffee houses stood. Their customers were stockbrokers from the Royal Exchange. An account by a gentleman called Maitland, in 1756 described the then Exchange Alley as:

Shops wishing to sell tea had to display a licence known as having their 'letters up'. In 1750 there were 50,000. In 1800 there were 150,000 and by 1870 there were nearly 195,000.

> Known all over the Mercantile World on account of the Business there transacted in Money Affairs, this being the grand Market for buying and selling stocks, Lottery tickets, etc... Merchants, Brokers and other financiers, assembled here daily from all parts of Europe and distant Nations in pursuit of riches.

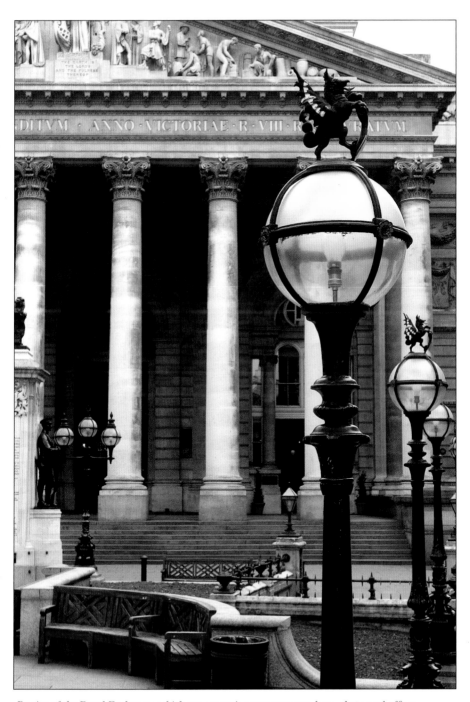

Portico of the Royal Exchange, which now contains a restaurant, bars, shops and offices.

11. Garraway's Coffee House

Continuing further into Change Alley, you will see a
plaque on the left showing the site of Jonathan's Coffee
House, while immediately opposite stood Sam's Coffee
House. As of 2005 the plaque is boarded up to protect
it from building work. By walking through Change
Alley turning left towards Birchin Lane, you come to
where Garraway's used to be on the first corner on
the right. There is a stone carving high up on the wall
to mark its location.

*Stone carving to
mark the site of
Garraway's*

Defoe in *A journey through England*, 1722, speaking
of the traders who went to the Royal Exchange wrote:
'But the better sort generally meet in the Exchange
Alley... At those celebrated coffee houses called Gar-
raway's... and Jonathan's... in the first, the people of
Quality, who have business in the City... and in
Jonathan's, the Buyers and Sellers of Stock...'

Mr Garraway had the distinction of opening the first coffee house after the 1666
Fire of London, which was on the site
of a Mr Elford's earlier coffee house. It
was Elford's father who was credited for
designing the first rotating coffee roaster.

In 1657 Garraway put up a poster in
his coffee house describing himself as
'Tobacconist and Retailer of Tea and
Coffee', but his claim to be the first to
introduce tea in England can be disputed,
because both beverages and chocolate were
being served in coffee houses from 1652.

*Detail of a receipt
of a tea and coffee
dealers*

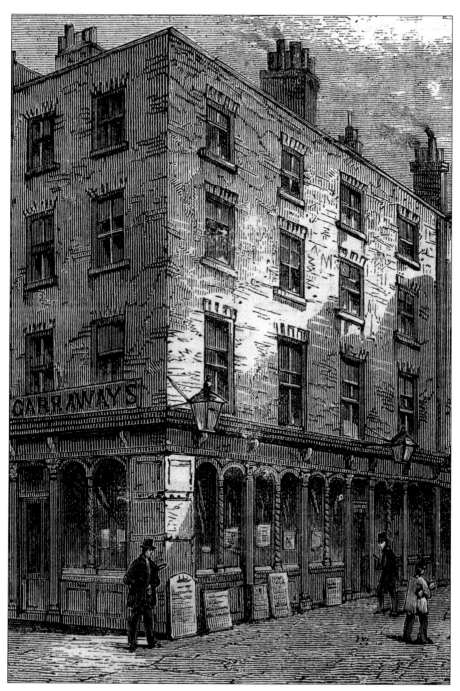

Garraway's coffee house, from a sketch taken shortly before demolition in 1846.

12. Sword Blade Coffee House

Continue down Change Alley until you reach the corner of Birchin Lane and Exchange Alley (now Change Alley). This is the site where the Sword Blade Coffee House stood.

Also to the right was Tom's, one of London's famous eighteenth century rendezvous for City merchants. Another of Tom's Coffee Houses, incidentally, was taken over by Mr Twining in 1717 before it moved to The Strand.

View of Birch's Coffee House, Cornhill

The map opposite shows the location of many of the old coffee houses before the fire of 1748, between Lombard Street and Cornhill. Between Exchange Alley and Birchin Lane there were another three coffee houses, the Rainbow, Jerusalem, and another Tom's, though these are not marked as you walk through.

Due to a shortage of small change in the late seventeenth century, coffee houses produced their own tokens. They could be exchanged for coffee, tea, chocolate and sherbet.

Designs of tokens from Coffee houses. The Sultanes in Cornhill and The Morat in Exchange Alley

Tom King's coffee house in the morning

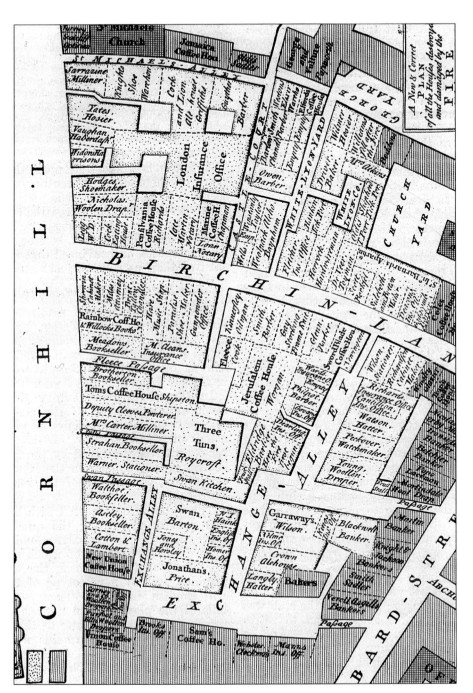

Plan of buildings in Cornhill destroyed by a fire which began in Exchange Alley in 1748.

East India Company, Tea and Opium

By 1760, Britain was importing some 4.5 million tons
of tea annually and finding the money to pay for it
was causing problems. Opium grown in India and
paid for in silver by the Chinese provided an answer.
The silver was credited against debts in London without the metal actually leaving China.

Opium had been grown in Sichuan in China for
centuries and the introduction of tobacco made it

easier to take. The Portuguese and the British added to these supplies, the first shipment reaching Macao in 1700.

The Chinese Government disapproved of the trade as demand and addiction grew. Edicts were issued as early as 1729 and importation was made illegal in 1800. However, the drug continued to be smuggled in, overseen by corrupt Chinese officials who were bribed by the British.

Britain rationalised the situation, with the popular opinion that opium had no more effect on the Chinese than beer or spirits had on the English trade, as it allowed India some economic self sufficiency.

Opium smokers in the east end of London, 1874

13. The George and Vulture

Turn left out of Change Alley, up Birchin Lane; the first alley on the right is a narrow passage, Bengal Court, only 40 inches wide. Take the second alley on the right into Castle Court which is also narrow. The Marine Coffee House used to stand on the left. Also on the left there is a little alleyway, Balls Court, leading to Simpson's Eating Room. Established in 1750, it is well worth a detour.

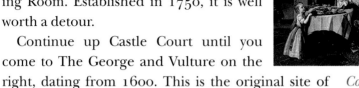

Continue up Castle Court until you come to The George and Vulture on the right, dating from 1600. This is the original site of Elford's Coffee House, built after the Great Fire. It leads into St Michael's Alley.

Conversation piece by Johann Zoffany, 1766

During the eighteenth century the names most circulated in the London Coffee Houses would have

included Samuel Johnson, Blackstone, Adam Smith and Smollett. Also painters like Joshua Reynolds and William Hogarth were in vogue with their conversation pieces, a British eighteenth-century genre which portrayed people sharing common activities such as having tea.

Left: Thomas Wentworth, Earl of Strafford, and his family taking tea, c. 1732, by Gawen Hamilton

Joseph Bramah Jr, the inventor, whose father was the coachman to the Earl of Strafford, and who lived on the estate, would undoubtedly have heard of the fashion for tea drinking, which certainly stimulated his interest in making the tea caddy shown on page 10.

The present George and Vulture.

14. Pasqua Rosee's Head

From the top of Castle Court you come to St Michael's Alley. There on the corner you will see the site of London's oldest coffee house, which was opened in 1652, at the sign of Pasqua Rosee's Head. It is now the site of the Jamaica Wine House though it was known for years as the Jamaica Coffee House.

Plaque indicating the site of Pasqua Rosee's Head

HERE STOOD
THE FIRST LONDON
COFFEE HOUSE
AT THE SIGN OF
PASQUA ROSEE'S HEAD
1652

Characters from a coffee house around 1720 by Hogarth

Although coffee has nearly as long a history as tea, it did not reach Europe until the seventeenth century. In England it was still a very novel beverage, when Daniel Edwards, a much travelled merchant, who had trading connections with Turkey, brought supplies of coffee back with him to London. Finding that his house was seldom free of guests who wanted to try the new drink, he arranged for his servant Pasqua Rosee, whom he had brought from Turkey, to prepare and serve coffee to offer it for sale to the public. It began a social revolution which swept all London, a revolution which was to repeat itself in the coffee bar era three centuries later.

Site of the Jamaica Coffee House

Site of the Pasqua Rosee's Head.

15. St Michael's Church

Turn up St Michael's Alley keeping the Jamaica Wine House on your right. On the corner of St Michael's Alley as you come into Cornhill is St Michael's Church. Turn right into Cornhill and walk towards Leadenhall Street.

It is fortunate that the City authorities have been able to retain the little alleyways between the buildings between Cornhill and Lombard Street. You feel on every paving stone that generations of traders have walked this way. The whole area is permeated with character and one can imagine the scene inside the coffee houses.

In the winter months, patrons would have found the fires inside the coffee rooms a welcome respite from the cold. Smoke from these fires would have mingled with tobacco smoke from clay pipes, and the aroma of coffee being roasted and brewed. As the evening wore on, the light of the oil lamps and candles would have been diminished by the thickening atmosphere, so that it would have been more difficult to read the broadsides, newspapers, or rules of the house, thoughtfully provided by the proprietors.

View of St Michael's Church, Cornhill, with the Jamaica Coffee House on the left, 1811

It is quite possible that if the coffee houses had not antedated the public sale of tea by a few years, these coffee meeting places would have been known as tea houses.

The entrance to St Michael's Church today.

16. Leadenhall Market

Cross Gracechurch Street into Leadenhall Street, take the first turning on the right, Whittington Avenue, which leads into Leadenhall Market. The market extended from Leadenhall Street to Lime Street. Shoppers in the market could often hear the shouts of bidding for teas from the auction room of the East India House which was next door and is now the site of Lloyds Insurance.

There has been an indoor food market here since the Middle Ages and its name derives from a lead roofed house that stood close by in the fourteenth century. The indoor market in Victorian style was designed in 1881 by Sir Horace Jones. The speciality of the market is poultry and game and it would be difficult to find an area which has such an image of quality food presentation.

The market calls to mind the atmosphere of *The Forsyte Saga* by John Galsworthy. You can imagine Jolyon the teaman attending the auctions in the East India house next door. Indeed, auctions must have leant to the sense of occasion for the shoppers, and have reminded them to add tea to their shopping list to take home for Christmas.

Lyons' range of teas 'for every pocket'.

The present Leadenhall market.

The East India Company

Although the East India Company received its char-
ter in 1600, it took 50 years for the British to take
up the habit of tea drinking. Tea was already avail-
able in Holland and when it came to Britain it was
sold in apothecary shops before it attracted
the attention of the coffee
house   keepers,

who started to market as well as sell it. Tea was the first commodity to be advertised in a London newspaper when the Sultan's Head Coffee House in Aldersgate Street, north of St Paul's Cathedral, announced its availability at its premises. This advertisement must have attracted as much attention as the news that Catherine of Braganza who married Charles II in 1662 was a tea drinker. Indeed, the first thing she asked for when she landed in Portsmouth was a cup of tea.

East India Company House around 1875

Advanced technology has put people on the moon. They went there and back in five days, but voyages in the early 1600s were a journey into the unknown, and early navigators were often away for years and had no guarantee they were going to return.

17. Site of East India House

Retrace your steps back up Whittington Avenue and turn right back into
Leadenhall Street. Shortly on your
right you will see the Lloyds Insurance
building. This was the site of the East
India Company Building.

The aquatint on the right shows
a tea auction taking place in the sale
room at the East India House in 1808.
The grandeur of the surrounding suggested that tea   *Receipt for*
was a profitable trade to be in. This aquatint and the   *Souchong and*
print on the previous page gives some idea of the status   *Green Tea, 1792*
that the East India Company enjoyed in its heyday.
The building in fact became one of the show places
of London. In the City, banking is business, tea and
coffee are trade and the tea trade has always held an
aristocratic position in the world of buying and selling. This view gathered substance through the huge
profits that the East India Company ships were able
to attain on some of their voyages.

The directors also enjoyed taking tea. In 1670 Lord
Berkeley started the tradition of giving colleagues a tea
set as a gift on special occasions. The auctions themselves were frequently unruly, with much howling and
yelling as the bidding advanced farthing by farthing,
until the uproar became quite frightening. The sales   *Teapot resembling*
were held four times a year: March, June, September   *a coffee pot pre-*
and December.   *sented in 1670*

At the turn of the eighteenth century, the East India   *to the Committee*
Company often had some 500,000 hundred pound   *of the East India*
chests of China tea in store and the auctions would   *Company*
sell 12,000 lots of these chests in a single day. It was
the greatest tea company the world had ever known.

The Sale Room at the East India House, 1808.

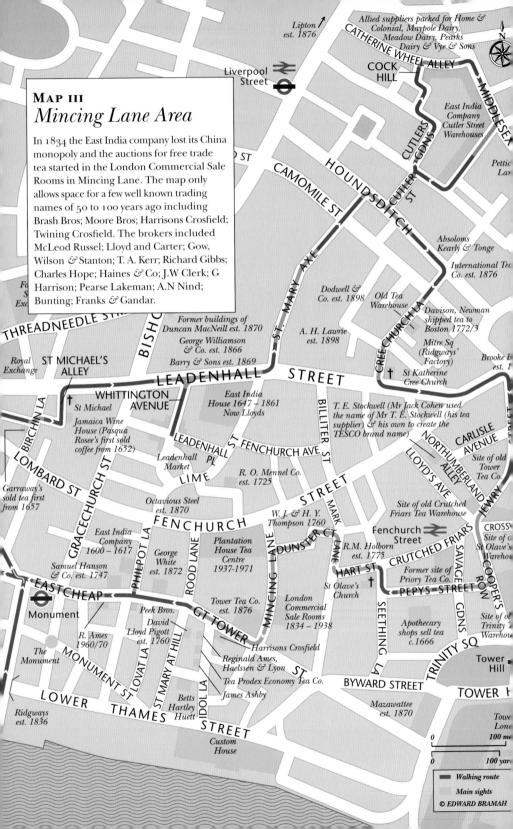

MAP III
Mincing Lane Area

In 1834 the East India company lost its China monopoly and the auctions for free trade tea started in the London Commercial Sale Rooms in Mincing Lane. The map only allows space for a few well known trading names of 50 to 100 years ago including Brash Bros; Moore Bros; Harrisons Crosfield; Twining Crosfield. The brokers included McLeod Russel; Lloyd and Carter; Gow, Wilson & Stanton; T. A. Kerr; Richard Gibbs; Charles Hope; Haines & Co; J.W Clerk; G Harrison; Pearse Lakeman; A.N Nind; Bunting; Franks & Gandar.

N

Lipton est. 1876

Liverpool Street

Allied suppliers packed for Home & Colonial, Maypole Dairy, Meadow Dairy, Pearks Dairy & Vye & Sons

CATHERINE WHEEL ALLEY

COCK HILL

East India Company Cutler Street Warehouses

MIDDLESEX

Pettic Lan

CUTLERS GDNS

CUTLER ST

HOUNDSDITCH

CAMOMILE ST

Absoloms Kearly & Tonge

International Tea Co. est. 1876

THREADNEEDLE ST

BISHO

Former buildings of Duncan MacNeill est. 1870
George Williamson & Co. est. 1866
Barry & Sons est. 1869

ST. MARY AXE

Dodwell & Co. est. 1898

Old Tea Warehouse

Davison, Newman shipped tea to Boston 1772/3

A. H. Lawrie est. 1898

CREE CHURCH LA

Mitre Sq (Ridgways' Factory)

Brooke B est. 1

Fo S Exc

Royal Exchange

ST MICHAEL'S ALLEY

LEADENHALL STREET

St Katherine Cree Church

WHITTINGTON AVENUE

St Michael

East India House 1647 – 1861 Now Lloyds

BILLITER ST

T. E. Stockwell (Mr Jack Cohen used the name of Mr T. E. Stockwell (his tea supplier) & his own to create the TESCO brand name)

CARLISLE AVENUE

NORTHUMBERLAND ALLEY

Site of old Tower Tea Co.

Jamaica Wine House (Pasqua Rosee's first sold coffee from 1652)

LEADENHALL PL

FENCHURCH AVE

BIRCHIN LA

LEADENHALL ST

LIME

Leadenhall Market

R. O. Mennel Co. est. 1725

STREET

LLOYD'S AVE

Site of old Crutched Friars Tea Warehouse

JEWRY

LOMBARD ST

GRACECHURCH ST

Garraway's sold tea first from 1657

Octavious Steel est. 1870

FENCHURCH

W. J. & H. Y. Thompson 1760

MARK LANE

Fenchurch Street

CROSSW

Site of St Olave's Wareho

East India Company 1600 – 1617

PHILPOT LA

George White est. 1872

ROOD LANE

Plantation House Tea Centre 1937-1971

DUNSTER CT

R.M. Holborn est. 1775

CRUTCHED FRIARS

SAVAGE

Samuel Hanson & Co. est. 1747

St Olave's Church

Former site of Priory Tea Co.

GDNS

COOPER'S ROW

Site of Trinity Wareho

EASTCHEAP

Peek Bros.

HART ST

PEPYS STREET

TRINITY SQ

Monument

R. Ames 1960/70

David Lloyd Pigott est. 1760

LOVAT LA

ST MARY AT HILL

GT TOWER

MINCING LANE

London Commercial Sale Rooms 1834 – 1938

SEETHING LA

Apothecary shops sell tea c.1666

Site of Trinity Wareho

The Monument

MONUMENT ST

Tower Tea Co. est. 1876

Harrisons Crosfield

Tower Hill

Reginald Ames, Haelssen & Lyon

BYWARD STREET

TOWER H

Ridgways est. 1836

LOWER THAMES

Betts Hartley Huett

IDOL LA

Tea Prodex Economy Tea Co.

James Ashby

STREET

Mazawattee est. 1870

Towe Lone

Custom House

0   100 me

0   100 yar

■■ Walking route

Main sights

© EDWARD BRAMAH

The tea trade is inextricably linked with Mincing Lane. Atmosphere is created in this extract
as a precursor to the information on page 86.

Morning in Mincing Lane (1864)

Paraphrased from one of the three anonymous articles, 'Up and Down the Lane',
which appeared in the *Grocer*, December 17, 1864, and subsequent issues.

Morning in Mincing Lane. A few old mansions are still left, but
the more recent structures are drab and utilitarian. Into this rather
sordid environment erupt, from nine o'clock onwards, the spruce
young broker and still sprucer brokers's clerks, stepping briskly
down the Lane with flowers in their buttonholes and their hair sym-
metrically parted in divisions as lustrous as their varnished boots.
By ten o'clock, dog–carts and smart gigs, and even an occasional
sober brougham, deliver some of the senior men, though most of
them travel by omnibus from the termini. Finally, by eleven, the sol-
emn, staid, high–dried and shabby heads of firms make their appear-
ance. These are the men who have 'risen from nothing', or have been
'put on a good thing by their friends', or have themselves 'put no
end of money into the concern'.

Mingling with the teamen, but distinguishable from them, are the
sugar brokers. You can tell them by their looser coats and lighter
waistcoats and their more florid, solid and jocular demeanour. The
handlers of tea, by contrast, are sharper, more subdued, with enquir-
ing noses, alert manners and general neatness.

Is it a fancy or have some of them that forced expression of repose,
that sallow fixity of expression, those dark–ringed eyes which
belong to the East?

18. St Mary Axe

Now turn off Leadenhall Street into St Mary Axe, nearly opposite Lloyds. It is a street well known in the old London tea trade. This street is a direct route between East India House at the southern end and the company's warehouses at the northern end on Cutler Street. At the height of the Victorian tea trade, a plethora of tea companies were located on the street. The plantation and agency houses, the tea brokerage companies and merchants, all had offices here.

THE BALTIC EXCHANGE

The Baltic Exchange building was destroyed by an IRA bomb attack in 1993, and their offices were replaced by the Swiss Re Tower. The Exchange offices are now next door in St Mary Axe.

This mercantile shipping exchange, whose function is the booking of cargoes in merchant vessels, was founded in its modern form in 1903, following the amalgamation of the Baltic Club with the London Shipping Exchange. Originally, business was done at the Virginia and Baltick (sic) coffee house, so called because the bulk of the freight came from America and the Baltic countries. Cargoes were auctioned in the saleroom provided on the premises, and in the coffee room captains and merchants were supplied with newspapers and kept informed of trading developments.

The largest warehouses in London, Horniman's in Wormwood St

Later, as business increased, the Antwerp Tavern in Threadneedle Street was purchased and renamed the Baltic Coffee House.

Home & Colonial Agency sign

The present Baltic Exchange.

The Docks

In the 1790s the extensive pilfering of cargo, particularly sugar and rum, from the ships using the Pool of London (see page 24) encouraged the West India Company to start the building of two dock basins 3 ½ miles down river near Blackwall. They were completed in two years, by 1802 with locks, warehouses and surrounding walls.

It was inevitable that the powerful East India Company with its great Cutler Street Warehouses should construct its own enclosed new docks. Its ships were the largest using the river and many were built at nearby Blackwall Shipyard. Again the docks were built speedily and they were opened in 1806.

The docks had no enclosed storage. Instead, 60 carriages, each capable of carrying 50 chests of tea, were used to transport tea, by road, to the Cutler Street Warehouses. The company paid £10,000 towards the cost of the creation of East India Dock Road and the Commercial Road.

Dockers at work, unloading a cargo of tea, 1880

19. Cutler Street Warehouses

From St Mary Axe, walk across Camomile Street and Houndsditch (look across the road to your right) into Cutler Street. Cutler Street leads through the gates into the warehouse complex (closed Saturdays and Sundays), just east of where Liverpool Street Station is presently situated.

Below left: view of the East India Company's warehouses from Cutler Street, 1836

These warehouses were built to keep the cargoes brought from the East India Docks near Blackwall. It was arranged to bring cargoes to London by using horse drawn wagons on the specially constructed Commercial Road in 1804. This was all done in order to avoid the considerable pilferage that existed on the river.

The building of the Cutler Street Warehouses began in 1770 and took thirty years to complete. It was in the Cutler Street Warehouses and in other warehouses in Crutched Friars that 4,000 warehousemen and 400 clerks were responsible for handling the company's tea stocks.

The Cutler Street Warehouses were an enormous, imposing structure with cranes and pulleys that would have been used to manoeuvre goods.

Views of the Cutler Street Warehouses

Cutlers Gardens is now a modern complex with offices.

20. Petticoat Lane (Middlesex Street)

By walking into the warehouse complex through the Cutlers Gardens entrance (weekdays only), you will wonder at the sheer size of the great buildings. Different commodities were stored in different buildings, tea usually being in warehouse No 6. The atmosphere of Cock Hill and Catherine Wheel Alley is evocative of past trading, as are gates 18 and 21 and the East India warehouse entrance on the corner of Petticoat Lane located on Middlesex Street.

Warehouse No 6, where tea was stored

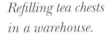

Refilling tea chests in a warehouse.

Many thousands of visitors to this famous lane must walk past these warehouses without realising they once stored China tea for the East India Company.

Typical inside labelling from a new season tea 'per first steamer'

In the warehouses, the smell of tea was quite pungent and the dust was everywhere.

The Boston Tea Party

The 1765 Stamp Act introduced a levy in the American
Colonies on certain imports.

 After protests by the Colonists, the Government
abandoned the duties except for its tax of 3d for
each pound on tea. The East
India Company with a sur-
plus of tea, found the competition of smuggling to
America from Holland
so great, it secured

The Boston Tea Party as it occurred: by night

the help of Parliament which passed the 1773 Tea Act. This allowed teas to be shipped to America without payment of English duty, but the tea retained the 3 pence colonial tax. Although this effectively lowered the price of tea to the colonists, it implied the British Parliament's power to raise revenue without any form of parliamentary representation.

Consequently 342 chests of tea were thrown overboard, a boycott of all British goods was organised and the British introduced Martial law.
War and the Declaration of Independence followed.

21. The Old Tea Warehouse

From the East India Company warehouses, trace your steps back to Houndsditch, where you turn left. Cross the road and walk down Houndsditch until you come to Creechurch Lane on your right.

Satirical drawing 'A Good Cup of Tea (When the duty is taken off)' by George Cruik- shank, 1848

At the far end on the left of the lane is an attractive old pub called The Old Tea Ware- house, which commemorates the Boston Tea Party and the history of one of the companies that supplied the tea to America.

The firm, Davison, Newman & Co., established in 1769, shipped tea to Boston in 1772 and 1773, the year of the memorable party, which started the Amer-

Co-operative Wholesale Society: tea estate, picking, consignment, shipping, packing machine and tea in the home

ican War of Independence, resulting in the founding of the United States of America.

This company traced its roots from Daniel Rowlinson, who was a friend of Samuel Pepys. He had established himself in 1650 as the proprietor of one of the many Mitre Taverns. The shop sign for Davison, Newman & Co. was a Crown and Three Sugar Loaves.

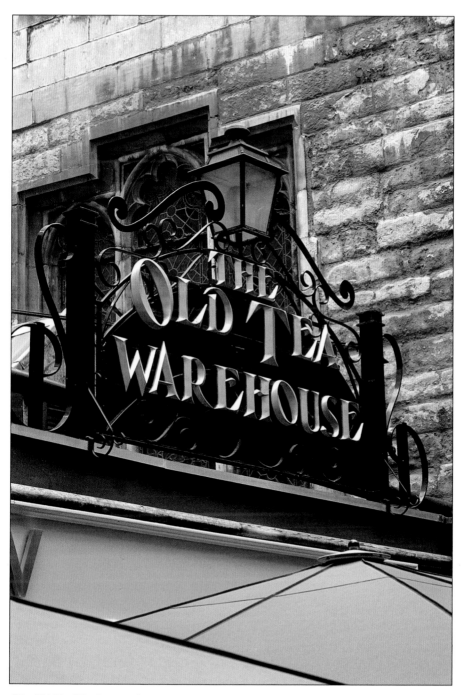

The Old Tea Warehouse pub.

The Adulteration of Tea

It was undoubtedly the tea damaged whilst being brought from ship to shore, or in storage whilst being smuggled, that created the notion of re-forming or treating leaf tea from China.

In around 1730 a practice of mixing tea with liquorice and sloe leaves and then staining the mixture with terra japonica, logwood, clay, molasses, and sugar to achieve artificial colour had developed. This is an account of the sort of method employed:'The leaves are gathered, dried in the sun and then baked. They are next put on the floor and trod upon until the leaves are small, then lifted and steeped in copperas, with sheep's dung, after which, being dried on a floor, they are fit for use.'

In an article by Dr Hill Hasal that appeared in *The Times* in 7 January 1874 one can read: 'I have made further analysis of the teas generally sold.

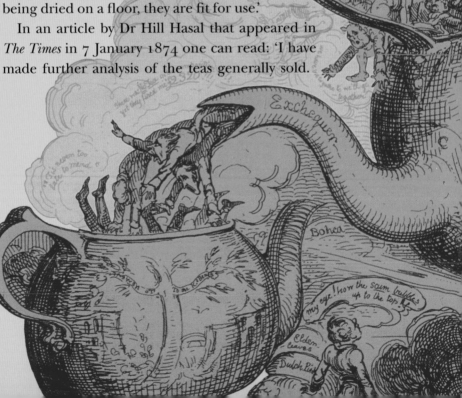

Of 18 samples, all were found adulterated and artificially coloured.'

In 1784 the malpractice was brought to public attention and a fine of £10 for every pound was enforced.

Satirical illustration showing the tea trade in hot water over the matter of adulteration.

22. Jewry Street Tea Factories

From the bottom of Creechurch Lane, you continue the Bramah Walk by turning round the corner of St Katharine Cree, a pre-Wren seventeenth century church, into Leadenhall Street. Keeping on walking you will come into Aldgate, from which across the road on the right you will see Jewry Street.

Teas and coffees were usually advertised on matchboxes

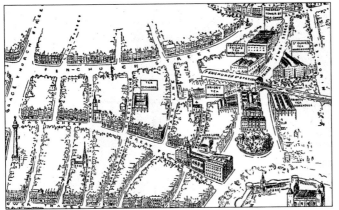

Tea companies in Jewry Street, 1889

In Jewry Street in 1890 there were three enormous tea warehouses. On the right, in the area between Carlisle Avenue and Northumberland Alley was the Great Tower Street Tea Company, later known as the Tower Tea Company. Further down the road, also on the right, as far as Lloyd's Avenue was Crutched Friars Tea Warehouse, while opposite, on the left, between Crutched Friars and Crosswall, was St Olave's Tea Warehouse.

Typical advertisement by the Tower Tea Company

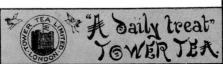

Advertisement by the Tower Tea Company.

23. Pepys Street Area

From Jewry Street, walk under the railway bridge down Cooper's Row. On your right is Trinity House, which was the site of the Trinity Tea Warehouse. Retrace your steps a few yards back up Coopers Row and turn left into Pepys Street. The street was named after the famous diarist. Later in 1667 he noted that the apothecary had recommended tea to his wife for her cold. While walking along Pepys Street, you pass the former site of the Priory Tea Company.

When Samuel Pepys took up his appointment as Secretary to the Admiralty Commission in 1673 and wrote in his diary 'I did send for a cup of tea, (a China drink), of which I had never drunk before,' he would have had little difficulty getting it. After all he lived literally in the middle of an area where tea was landed, stored, mixed, bought, and sold. Certainly, the streets all around him were to become, for a period of three hundred years, right up to the bomb damage of World War II, the centre of the UK tea trade.

Samuel Pepys by John Hayls, 1666

Pepys enjoyed the drink in his office in the same way the directors of the East India Company found tea too valuable for use at 'The Court of Committees'. They sent out for six to eight pounds of tea at a time, which they bought from the coffee house keepers. Meanwhile Mrs Pepys had bought tea leaf from the apothecary for making at home. Pepys was a visitor to many of the City coffee houses where it would be customary for the tea to be infused, stored in kegs to be drawn off and heated as required. The customs officer would measure the taxable drinkables before they were sold.

Detail of a London coffee dealer receipt

Sole Agents to the London Colonial Coffee Mart.

Advertisement by the United Kingdom Tea Company depicting Samuel Pepys, 1894.

24. St Olave's Church

Turning right at the end of Pepys Street onto Seething Lane is the side entrance to the delightful church
of St Olave, which stood in the middle of tea trading
on the north side of the River Thames. The main
entrance to the church is on Hart Street.

Almost one thousand years ago, at the battle of London Bridge, King Olave of Norway fought the Danes.
Olave, who became a saint, was a seafaring man, and
the church has had strong seafaring connections
since early in the eleventh century. The church was
rebuilt in the thirteenth century and again in the
fifteenth century. It survived the Great Fire, but was
damaged in World War II.

*The altar and east
window*

Samuel Pepys and his wife are buried here (you
can also find a memorial on the south wall) and there
is, inside the chapel, a statue of the couple. Many
victims are mentioned in the burial register including Mary Ramsey, who is said to have
brought the Plague to London.

*Statue of Sir Andrew
Riccard, chairman
of the East India
Company*

The church, being at the eastern end
of the City, was almost in the centre of
the tea trading area and, like St Michael's,
many tea people would have gone through
its doors. No doubt many of the East India
Company staff such as Sir Andrew Riccard
were buried here as were also the tea dealers
Mr Davison and Mr Newman.

The crypt of St Olave's dates from around 1250.

25. Mincing Lane Tea Auctions

Turn right onto Hart Street, pass St Olave's and turn right onto Mark Lane, then by walking through Dunster Court (open office hours) on the left you come

into Mincing Lane, famous for its tea auctions. On weekends you can get to the other side of Dunster Court by walking up Mark Lane to Fenchurch Street and then turning left into Mincing Lane.

Catalogue for an auction in 1838

Above left: offices at a tea company.

Left: mixing teas together in a circular revolving drum to create blends and weighing tea from chests into packets

On the left, going south, were the London Commercial Sale Rooms, built in 1811. The trade held its auctions there from 1834.

The catalogue depicted on the right is from a tea auction held on 2 April 1838. The teas for sale were all China teas. This was the year before Indian tea first came to the UK market.

Mr C. E. Irving, a Mincing Lane tea taster of the 1930s considers the blend that he is sampling.

Auctions

The auctions were held in East India House for 156 years, and then in the London Commercial Sale Rooms building in Mincing Lane for another hundred years before moving to Plantation House in 1937. The auction room was on the seventh and eighth floors with an impressive mansard type roof, twenty–one feet high, designed with raised seating for 250 people. It was so grand that it was called the Plantation House Auditorium. Special attention had to be given to the acoustics. The walls were made of acoustic slabs, and the auctioneers's rostrum had been moved more than once to find the best position. Around the room were shields—four of which we have in the Museum— bearing the brightly coloured coat of arms of the various producing countries. The ceiling was glass–panelled, suggesting that the room was open to the sky. With its high rostrum and rows of raked seats, it was very impressive.

Auction at Plantation House

Alas, by 1971, due to the contraction in the trade, the auctions left Mincing Lane and moved to Sir John Lyon House and finally to the London Chamber of Commerce building in 1990 before they finally closed in 1998. Tea auctions had continuously been held, except during the world wars, for 319 years.

26. Plantation House

In 1937 the London Tea Auctions were transferred to Plantation House. It was situated across the road, on the corner of Mincing Lane and Fenchurch Street. These buildings were demolished in 2002.

In the mid nineteenth century, at least half of the tea being handled by brokers and buyers was blended and packed within two miles of the tea auction room in Mincing Lane.

Plantation House

Unfortunately the factories are too dispersed and numerous for this walk, but they include Lipton's on Bethnal Green Road; the Co–op in Leman Street and Brooke Bond in Goulston Street.

The remains of the Mazawattee factory on Tower Hill were destroyed during the war; Joseph Travers packed tea in St Katherine's Dock; and Ridgways packed tea in Shepherdess Walk. Both George Payne and Priory were south of the river, in Southwark.

When war broke out in 1939, the government in effect took over the tea trade. The tea auctions were suspended and tea, like other food such as butter, sugar, bacon and lard, was rationed. About thirty Thames side warehouses had their tea stocks distributed around the country to 500 different locations.

The shields of the
auction room at
Plantation House
are now in the
Bramah Museum

Catalogue of
an auction in
Plantation House

The London Commercial Sale Rooms, where the tea auctions were held for a century, 1860.

British Blenders

With the arrival of Indian and Ceylon teas in Britain, there was a dramatic decline in the demand for tea and, consequently, auctions held for China tea. The catalogue depicted on page 90 refers to an auction for China teas in Mincing Lane in 1958. The author endeavoured to breathe life into the China trade by arranging to have China tea offered for sale by auction on behalf of the Tea Corporation of the People's Republic of China. It was the first time the Chinese producers had put their tea in the London auctions themselves.

The prices fetched were modest enough, but from the selection offered, the 'blending type' teas, which the author had been campaigning for, were most successful, representing a step towards making China tea acceptable to the UK market.

Weekly auctions of China tea continued until February 1959, by which time 10,248 chests had been offered. The total added up to £73,823, the average selling price being slightly over 2 shillings per pound.

Typical 1950s advertisements by the largest UK tea blenders

A variety of stamps from tea growing countries

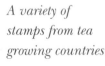

A variety of tea labels used by British blenders in the past. By the design it is possible to see the growing offer and demand for Indian and Ceylon teas

27. Eastcheap

At the bottom of Mincing Lane you come to Great
Tower Street (first recorded in the thirteenth century)
where, from 1823, the Moore Brothers traded at num-
bers 52 and 53. Turn right and walk along this street

*Cover of book of
an Eastcheap
tea trading
company*

*Mazawattee tea
advertisement*

until it becomes Eastcheap, where many firms trading
in tea had their premises. Hansons traded
from 1747 until 1947 and were famous for
their red, white and blue coffee and David
Lloyd Pigott were just off Eastcheap to
name but two. On the right you
pass Philpot Lane, the street in
which the East India Company
was founded. Continuing down
Eastcheap you will cross King
William Street and arrive in
Cannon Street.

*The Great
Tower Street
Tea Company
warehouses*

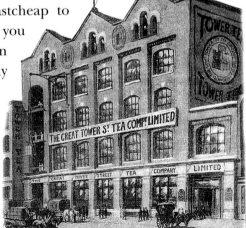

Peek House in Eastcheap used to be the headquarters of the Peek Brothers.

Decline of the Old Trading

Between World War I and World War II, most of Britain's tea was warehoused along both sides of the River Thames, between London Bridge and Deptford, and over half of the tea was blended and packed in the Pool of London area. In fact, with the advent of World War II, it was considered too dangerous to have so much of the same stock in one area, so that tea from nearly thirty warehouses was distributed to hundreds of other locations in different parts of the country. Nevertheless, when the bombs started to fall, over

The Pool of London after a bombing raid in World War II

eight thousand tons of teas were destroyed by fire and half of the tea brokers had their offices destroyed.

In the war, the auctions were suspended and tea was rationed to the public (at the rate of two ounces per person per week) until 1956. In the same year, the auctions were started again but the anticipated renaissance of the tea trade simply did not happen. Coffee bars and espresso coffee became popular with the younger people. Television promoted instant soluble coffee to millions of homes and the tea trade had to compete. Tea bags with a quick infusion were introduced.

Labour troubles also hit the London docks in the 1960s and the multi–storied buildings and narrow lanes of the river front did not lend themselves to the bulk pallet handling of tea. It was found easier to land the tea closer to the provincial packing factories.

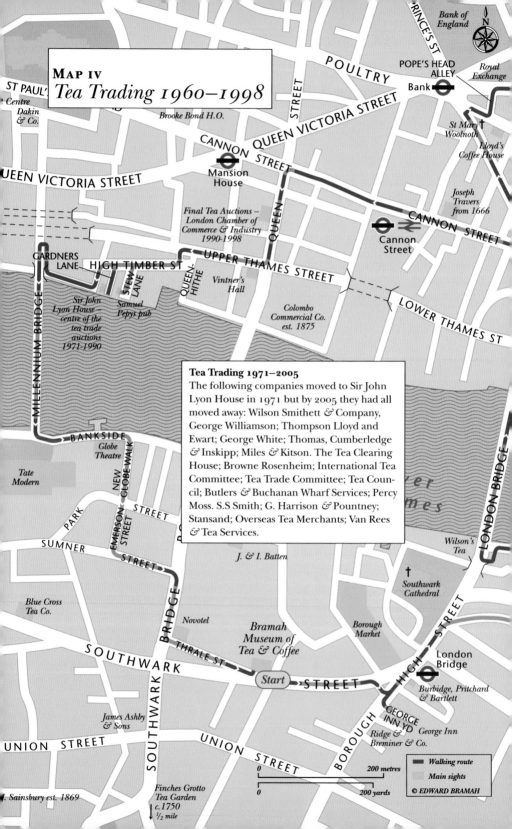

MAP IV
Tea Trading 1960–1998

PRINCE'S ST

Bank of England

N

POULTRY

POPE'S HEAD ALLEY

Royal Exchange

Bank

ST PAUL'

Centre Dakin & Co.

Brooke Bond H.O.

CANNON STREET

QUEEN VICTORIA STREET

St Mary Woolnoth

Lloyd's Coffee House

QUEEN VICTORIA STREET

STREET

Mansion House

Joseph Travers from 1666

CANNON STREET

Final Tea Auctions – London Chamber of Commerce & Industry 1990-1998

QUEEN

Cannon Street

GARDNERS LANE

HIGH TIMBER ST

UPPER THAMES STREET

STEW LANE

QUEEN-HITHE

Vintner's Hall

LOWER THAMES ST

MILLENNIUM BRIDGE

Sir John Lyon House – centre of the tea trade auctions 1971-1990

Samuel Pepys pub

Colombo Commercial Co. est. 1875

Tea Trading 1971–2005

The following companies moved to Sir John Lyon House in 1971 but by 2005 they had all moved away: Wilson Smithett & Company, George Williamson; Thompson Lloyd and Ewart; George White; Thomas, Cumberledge & Inskipp; Miles & Kitson. The Tea Clearing House; Browne Rosenheim; International Tea Committee; Tea Trade Committee; Tea Council; Butlers & Buchanan Wharf Services; Percy Moss. S.S Smith; G. Harrison & Pountney; Stansand; Overseas Tea Merchants; Van Rees & Tea Services.

BANKSIDE

Globe Theatre

NEW GLOBE WALK

Tate Modern

EMERSON STREET

STREET

er mes

LONDON BRIDGE

Wilson's Tea

SUMNER

PARK

STREET

J. & I. Batten

Southwark Cathedral

Blue Cross Tea Co.

Novotel

Bramah Museum of Tea & Coffee

Borough Market

London Bridge

BRIDGE

THRALE ST

Start

STREET

HIGH STREET

Burbidge, Pritchard & Bartlett

James Ashby & Sons

SOUTHWARK

BOROUGH

GEORGE INN YD

George Inn

Ridge & Breminer & Co.

UNION STREET

UNION STREET

. Sainsbury est. 1869

Finches Grotto Tea Garden c.1750

½ mile

0   200 metres

0   200 yards

■ *Walking route*

Main sights

© EDWARD BRAMAH

Orthodox Tea and Tea Bags

When China tea imports declined, the British were treated to 100 years of superb Indian and Ceylon machine–made teas.

This tea was so good that it supported the commercial foundations of the leading tea packaging companies we have known in the last century. Their blends required a 5 minute infusion which was the heart and soul of the English Afternoon Tea, a ceremony with its own etiquette. After the first pouring, more water was added to the tea in the teapot for a second serving.

In the 1960s, the tea trade, eager to compete with instant coffee changed its manufacturing procedure by putting the leaf through a new machine consisting of two horizontal rollers like a mangle, which crushed, tore and curled the leaf in a much quicker time than the traditional method of rolling tea in a circular drum. The result was a quick infusing tea, used in tea bags.

Tea bags today meet the demands of modern life and represent an important position in the supply of tea by the trade.

A recent survey showed that tea bags on average only stay in a mug or teapot for 30 seconds. This practice conspires against the fashion of British Afternoon Tea as we know it. Nevertheless, the connoisseur will always ask for orthodox tea, made the orthodox way, with tea leaves in a teapot and its incomparable taste.

28. Cannon Street

The walk continues over into Cannon Street where, at number 145 the tea firm Joseph Travers & Sons can trace its ancestry under various changes of name as far back as 1666. They handled teas for the East India Company, which was only down the road.

Explanation of marks used in tea auction catalogues

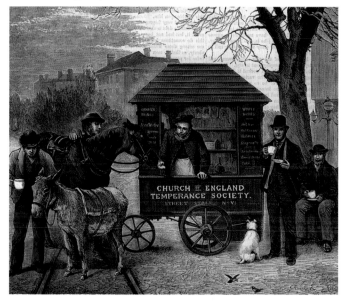

Coffee stall of the Temperance Society around 1890

More than a hundred years ago around this area we would have found tea and coffee stalls, which were open day and night and provided refreshment for workers. The picture above shows a stall of the Temperance Society.

The Temperance Movement, which began to make progress in the 1820s, was dedicated to promoting moderation and, more often, complete abstinence in the use of alcohol. In this respect it also encouraged the consumption of tea by charitable tea meetings.

'From East to West We bring the best O'er land and Sea Mazawattee'

Warming up with hot coffee on Blackfriars Bridge at 5 am (nineteenth century).

29. Last London Tea Auctions

After passing Cannon Street Station, on the corner with Queen Victoria Street, is the London Chamber of Commerce and Industry building. This building served as the site for tea auctions from 1990 until 1998 when the last tea auction was held, 319 years after the first tea auction.

View from Gardner's Lane in 2005

However, to see where the auctions were held from 1972 to 1990, proceed to the bottom of Queen Street and turn into Upper Thames Street. Walk past the Vintner's Hall so as to bear left down High Timber Street. Passing Stew Lane you might wish to take a detour to take in the atmosphere of the river by resting at the Samuel Pepys pub.

Continue to the next street beyond Stew Lane, Gardner's Lane. The auctions were held in a ground floor room overlooking the river in Sir John Lyon House, which was named after a sixteenth century Lord Mayor who had his warehouse there.

Site of the London Chamber of Commerce and Industry

However the Sir John Lyon House is being demolished in 2005 so, instead, take the next road, Broken Wharf, which leads to Paul's Wharf on the river front.

Catalogue of the last tea auction

Sir John Lyon House (left) prior to being demolished in 2005 and a refurbished warehouse.

30. The Tea Clearing House

Continue along Paul's Wharf until you arrive at the
steps of the Millennium Bridge, which will give you a
real feel for how important the river was for the trans-
portation of goods.

Alternatively, you can walk back to the Museum
directly over Southwark Bridge. To do this, walk past
Stew Lane to Queenhithe. This leads to the river and
the Thames Walk leads to the steps up onto the
bridge. Walk over the bridge and follow the signs.

*Clearing House
stamp*

An elderly tea trader writing in 1986 said: 'I feel I
saw the best of the tea trade when the auctions were
full of good–humoured banter. There were so many
buyers in those days and therefore so many more
interesting personalities'.

The Tea Clearing House, located in Sir John Lyon
House, did what its name implies: clearing the paper
work, enabling samples and documentation from the
various warehouses to be collected without a hold up
in the administration.

The idea came about in 1884 and was that of a
staff member with the Metropolitan Warehouse. As
a result, as many as 16 warehouses became members
and 200 dealers and brokers joined as subscribers.
In 1972 when many tea firms and the tea auctions
moved from Mincing Lane to Sir John Lyon House
the Tea Clearing House moved into a warehouse next
door.

*The original letter
with the draft of
the scheme for
the formation of
the Tea Clearing
House in London*

Edward Bramah (third from right, front row) in pensive mood during the last tea auction.

Modern Tea

The Millennium Bridge's very modernity provides a poignant contrast to the old tea trade buildings around the Pool of London. The new technology reinforces that one must move with the times.

The bridge provides a chance to stand in the middle of the river and admire the magnificent views of the river fronts, which had contained many of the tea warehouses.

We are reminded that external influences have always triggered change. From East Indiamen to clipper ships; clippers to steam; roasted coffee to liquid essence and on to soluble powder; telegraph to telex and on to e–mail.

The sheer power of television led to modern marketing, creating new fashions that were

quickly taken up. The UK public in the 1950s would not have believed that 95% of people in the early twenty–first century would be using tea bags and that the public would not be aware that the tea made to go in them would be manufactured by a new crush, tear and curl (CTC) method, which makes brewing quicker.

A grocer's shop at Christmas, 1850

31. Millennium Bridge

As you walk over the Millennium Bridge, looking back at St Paul's Cathedral, you could reflect on how many cups of tea and coffee Sir Christopher Wren may have enjoyed to help him design his 52 churches! Maybe

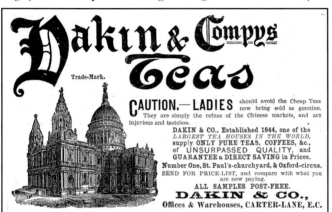

some enterprising tea maker prepared drinks for the labourers. This may have been the beginning of the Dakin tea company whose address was Number One, London, St Paul's Churchyard.

A range of typical tea company advertisements from the past

The Millennium Bridge and St Paul's Cathedral.

32. Tate Modern & Sugar Cubes

The enormous brick structure ahead of you as you cross the Millennium Bridge is Tate Modern, originally built as a power station, now home to a major collection of modern and contemporary art. The original Tate Galleries were created by Sir Henry Tate, who began trading in sugar in 1859.

Sir Henry built a large refinery that enabled the sugar to be cleaned and purified more effectively and in 1879 became the licensee of the Langen Patent and developed a new process of making sugar into cubes.

The Prince of Wales (left) and Mr Henry Tate enjoying a cup of tea

Before sugar cubes were invented, sugar was made in loaves, and needed to be broken into small pieces. The ladies used sugar nips to put the lumps elegantly in their tea.

Thus the sugar cube was a great boon and Mr Tate would have realised that the market for selling sugar was for making cubes to use in tea and coffee.

Sugar cutter, Bramah Museum

Advertisement for Mazawattee tea and coffee

The Tate Modern at Bankside.

Fine Traditional British Tea

The Chinese had a tea ceremony which the Japanese turned into an art form. Likewise, the Ethiopians have created a coffee culture which has become the basis of all domestic coffee–making.

If the British, in order to make tea, use freshly boiled water, heat the pot, infuse the leaf for five minutes, put the milk in the cup first, pour the tea through a strainer, top up the teapot with hot water for a second pouring, and use a tea cosy throughout, then that is also a tea ceremony. In fact, this is the ceremony of English afternoon tea, which the British popularised throughout the world and, in recent years, have taken too much for granted. The Museum reminds visitors of this 350 year old custom, especially, as the English tea ceremony and culture is worth pre-serving in its original form, using orthodox tea.

The British also played a key part in the develop-ment of a culture of coffee–making. British silver and ceramic coffee pots were famous in the nineteenth and twentieth centuries, as were also British biggins, percolators, steam, vacuum and siphon machines. Along with demitasse cups, cream, liqueurs and mints, they are part of an English coffee ceremony, culture and heritage.

Will the English Afternoon Tea Ceremony come back again? We do not like to think of it as a fashion, which comes and goes. Nationally, the state of a nation's economy decrees what we all do. Afternoon teas and the tea dance were introduced in the Victo-rian era when the country was rich. Today, the rich American market discovered the quality of real tea and the American people are becoming masters of the English tea ceremony using orthodox teas.

The value of a non-alcoholic social custom is obvious. The English tea ceremony is already back.

Afternoon tea under difficulties aboard ship, 1893

33. The Globe Theatre

Walk towards the Globe Theatre (the river will be on your left). In doing so, you will see the site opposite where, as already related, the tea auctions were held for almost twenty years before finally closing in 1998.

NEW GLOBE WALK SE1
BANKSIDE

At the Globe Theatre you have two alternative routes for returning back to the Bramah Museum. The first alternative is to continue along the river to Southwark Bridge where you walk up the steps to Southwark Bridge Road. Turn right at the top and follow the signs.

The second way to the Bramah Museum from the Globe would be to turn right into New Globe Walk. It is sad to walk away from the River Thames and its tea related history for over 350 years, but further references on the way back to the Bramah Museum tell us about tea at home and the famous London tea gardens, examples being Vauxhall and Finches Grotto. New Globe Walk runs into Emerson Street, at the end of which you turn left into Sumner Street. Walk to the end and turn right into Southwark Bridge Road.

John Bull, the character who epitomises Britain, having a cup of tea

Entrance to the Globe Theatre.

34. London's Terraced Houses

At the end of Sumner Street before turning right into Southwark Bridge Road, it is fun to look across the street at the sight of 50 chimney pots on the building opposite. Such houses were built in the early 1800s when tea was at the height of fashion. Every house would have had tea making equipage and of course every family in each house would have needed to keep fires alight to heat the range and boil the water

The family tea interrupted by news from the paper

for making tea. The Clean Air Act only came into effect after World War II. Before that, London was decidedly dirty, suffering from the smoke that belched out from thousands of London chimneys .

The picture above shows a typical British nineteenth-century household. The family sits by the fireside to enjoy their cups of tea. The lady on the left is reading the paper while the man standing by the fire is making the tea.

Above and below: old tea boxes and tins

The characteristic chimney pots of London's terraced houses.

Tea Gardens

Tea gardens, which were places of entertainment for Londoners of every class, were entirely indigenous to England and almost exclusively so to London.

Coming after the London Coffee Houses, they were popular during the 1700s and did more to popularise the 'new China drink' and afternoon tea than any other single factor. They spread from Bayswater to Stepney and out to Kilburn, Belsize, Hampstead, Hornsey and Dalston. Many were sited adjacent to springs, and water from several, such as the Dog and Duck Tea Garden in Mayfair, was offered for sale at the Golden Sheaf in Tavistock Street.

The best known tea gardens were Marylebone, Ranelagh and Vauxhall. The Vauxhall Tea Garden was spread over eleven acres, and had many attractions which included acrobats, balloon ascents, conjurors, deer hunting, equestrianism, fire–eaters, golf, jugglers, leap-frog, masquerade balls, nine pins, plunging baths, racquets, sliding on ice, tightrope dancers and waterfalls.

Other tea gardens included Islington and Bagnigge Wells in Clerkenwell, where buns, bread and butter, almond cheesecakes and tea were in abundance.

Promenading along the lime tree walks was fashionable amongst the ladies, and entertainments included orchestras, fireworks and illuminations. Equally popular were bathing, duck hunting, pigeon shooting and cricket.

View of the Grand Walk in Vauxhall Gardens with elegantly dressed figures strolling throughout the area, c.1750

35. Finches Grotto

Although not on this walk, it is interesting to note that within a mile of the Bramah Museum further down the Southwark Bridge Road was a pub named Finches Grotto, which was known for its tea garden. Many early gardens were connected to taverns as ale was, at the time, the universal English drink before the arrival of tea. No fewer than 85 tea gardens became established around London.

View of the Vauxhall Gardens, 1751

After the Great Plague in 1665, when around 70,000 people died, and the Great Fire of 1666, a new appreciation as to the importance of walking in the fresh air brought people out to the gardens surrounding London. Between Vauxhall and Southwark there were 16 tea gardens. Following the austere years of the Commonwealth and the Restoration of Charles II in 1660, there was a new mood for Londoners who demanded entertainment, which the tea gardens provided.

Detail of an eighteenth century receipt

Teas genuine as Imported.

Coffees & Spices of all kinds.

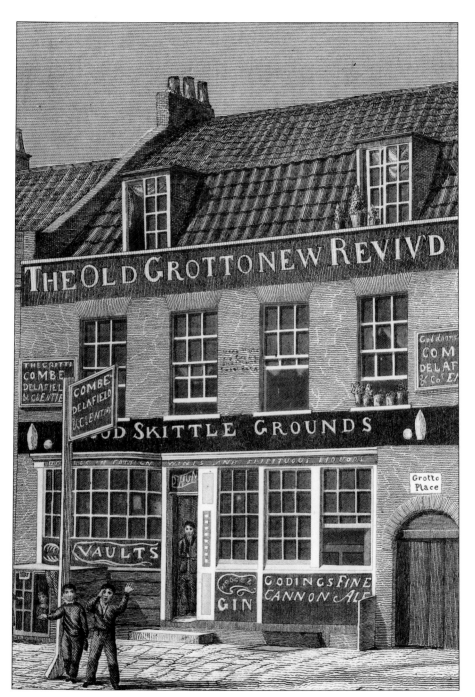

The Finches Grotto pub and tea garden in the early nineteenth century.

36. Thrale Street

Just beyond the corner of Southwark Bridge Road and Southwark Street is the Novotel hotel on Thrale Street.

Mrs Thrale was, for years, the owner of the nearby Thrale's Brewery. She was also a friend of Dr Johnson, one of Britain's most famous tea drinkers. From 1765 for over twenty years, they often had afternoon tea together, as witnessed from one of their tea parties, a picture of which is shown in the Bramah Museum.

Dr Johnson's addiction made him very impatient when he asked for leaves and water. His calls for these ingredients were constant. After preparing the pot, he swallowed the tea with haste. According to his own description, he was 'a hardened and shameless tea drinker, who has for twenty years diluted his meals with only the infusion of this fascinating plant; whose kettle scarcely has time to cool; who with tea amuses the evening, with tea solaces the midnight, and with tea welcomes the morning'.

The picture on the facing page epitomises the culture of the English afternoon tea ceremony, which the Bramah Museum stands for. In today's modern life it is easy for old customs and culture to disappear. The primary purpose of the Bramah Museum and the walk is to remind people of the art and standards that the British brought to their tea and coffee making in London.

Walk down Thrale Street to Southwark Street and here on the left you will arrive back at the Bramah Museum where you can complete your Bramah Tea and Coffee Walk certificate and enjoy a well earned cup of tea.

Mrs Thrale's teapot, now part of Dr Johnson's House Trust Collection

'Tea's proper use is to amuse the idle, and relax the studious and dilute the full meals who cannot use exercise and will not use abstinence.'
Dr Johnson

Mrs Thrale and Dr Johnson (second left) at tea.

37. The Certificate

After completing the Bramah Walk you are invited to
have your certificate signed.

You can also enjoy a cream or afternoon tea, made
with the finest orthodox tea, helping you to relax and
reflect on this unique London experience.

*The Bramah London
Tea & Coffee Walk Certificate*

_____

*has completed the
Bramah London Tea & Coffee Walk*

*Date*_____

Stamp   Edward Bramah
Director of The Bramah Tea and Coffee Museum

Fine

Teas

Index

The wind rose up – the sun went down
Upon that CHINA SEA